the HEART of a GARDEN

D1540502

by

Jess Wynne

**Edited by
Martin Gaunt**

OSCHA

Published by
Oscha Digital Media Distribution Ltd
Carrick Business Centre, Commercial Road, Penryn, Cornwall TR10 8AR.

www.oscha.com
www.theheartofagarden.com

Copyright © Oscha Ltd 2007

All rights reserved. No part of this book may be reproduced by any means or in any form whatsoever without written permission from the publisher, except for brief quotations embodied in literary articles or reviews.

Photographic Team for Oscha Ltd:
Joanne Bradford, Katie Prescott, Matt Wright and Jess Wynne

Additional photography:
Page 65 Brown hare, 68 Red kite, 69 Kingfisher photography and copyright © Rob Chace, 2007
Page 137 picture 2 and 3 photography and copyright © Abbey House Gardens, 2007

Photographic Editor
Matt Wright

Designed by
Julian Pickett

Printed by
Chalvington Press Ltd
The Old Granary, Malpas Road, Truro, Cornwall, UK TR1 1QH.

Printed in England

Note: Readers are advised to be aware that some of the plants mentioned in this book have toxic, carcinogenic, or other dangerous properties. Independent professional medical advice should be sought by any individual who intends to consume or come in to close contact with any of the plants mentioned in this book.

For Margaret Wynne: thank you for all the support and encouragement over the years.

In memory of John Francis White. A better writer than myself, but with a similar sense of irreverence.

Contents

Introduction

We set out to produce a book and film that celebrates the natural environment, armed with not much more than a sense of fun. We are not gardening notables, and back in the dark days we would have struggled to name more than a dozen plants between us. With ignorance as our main qualification, we felt well placed to create something subtly different, something that might appeal to non-gardeners and gardeners alike.

It was easy to imagine that we would fail to please either in looking to satisfy both—that was the risk we took. If you find it presumptuous that we should write about a subject from an uninformed standpoint, we hope that you still find it within yourself to enjoy our representation of the natural environment. And with a bit of luck, we might at least encourage you to visit some great gardens.

One final thought. We are all now a trifle nerdy when it comes to horticulture, and get easily excited when racing each other to smugly name plants (especially if we know the Latin). So, by our own proviso, we can no longer claim to be the best people for the job. That said, we enjoyed ourselves so much, we are already planning the next volume—and it's going to be even bigger. So be concerned; be very concerned!

Happy reading and looking.

Martin Gaunt
Producer – the Heart of a Garden

THE ABBEY GARDEN, TRESCO

Tresco, Isles of Scilly, Cornwall

Dazzling   Pioneering   Alien   Secluded   Unforgettable

The Abbey Garden on Tresco is an anomaly; a real example of nature tamed and what can be achieved by sheer determination and vision. In 1834, Augustus Smith moved to Tresco in the Isles of Scilly, surveyed the barren treeless landscape, suffered the Atlantic gales and sea spray, and decided what he really wanted was a nice garden.

In the ruins of the 12th-century St Nicolas Priory, Smith placed his first plantings. As the garden expanded, he cleverly built up a shelter belt using trees such as the Monterey Pine to offer the protection necessary for its survival. Successive generations of Smith's family have added to the garden, which now covers 17 acres. One influential character in the annals of the garden's history was Major Arthur Dorrien-Smith—and, in fact, it will soon be the 100th anniversary of his adventurous plant hunting expedition to the Chatham Islands and New Zealand. Although these days the business of plant hunting is rather less dramatic—and probably a lot less damaging ecologically—seeds still arrive at the Abbey Garden from exotic destinations on a regular basis.

This is truly a microcosm of a garden, with over 20,000 plants from the Mediterranean, Australia and New Zealand, South Africa and South America. How could this possibly be a UK garden?

Certainly it is unlikely that such a garden could exist anywhere else in the UK but here. The predominantly mild climate on the Isles of Scilly is superbly beneficial for nurturing tender and exotic plants. Some of the tougher succulents such as the *Aeonium,* known cheerfully as Scilly Cabbage, seem to have escaped the confines of the garden and can now been found in all sorts of strange places on the islands, casually growing out of granite walls or on garage roofs like some sort of alien invader.

The shelter belt provides a microclimate within the garden, shielding the plants from the Scilly's strong westerly and south-westerly winds, yet enabling them to take advantage of the island's mild weather and relatively low rainfall. For head gardener Andrew Lawson, it was 'definitely' the 'incredible' range of plants that can be grown here that made a career at Tresco Abbey his ultimate ambition, 'We started coming over here when I was eleven...My parents are both keen

botanists, so they were already interested in the garden and I guess that's how I got introduced to it. When I was 14, I came over and did a week unpaid in the gardens just to see whether it was the sort of job I wanted to do, and when I came away I thought, "well there's an ambition—get to work in the Abbey Gardens!'"

Andrew has worked at the gardens now for about 22 years, but time hasn't dimmed his enthusiasm for the work; he is hugely knowledgeable about every aspect of the garden. He can reel off, without any hesitation, facts and statistics about Tresco Abbey, yet is clearly happiest when immersing himself in the practicalities of gardening. 'My role is very much a practical hands-on wheelbarrow and wellies gardener if you like,' he says with a laugh, 'and that's the way that I like it, sitting in an office would drive me crazy. I'd much rather be out getting wet and actually seeing the job being done!'

Andrew describes Tresco's range as being 'anything between 30 and 45 degrees latitude in both the north and southern hemisphere' and concludes that most temperate plants can grow at Tresco, but the lack of high temperatures means that they can not afford to stray too far into the field of tropical vegetation. Because the clement climate allows growth all year round, and due to the variety of southern hemisphere plants, this is a garden that can truly boast of interest and colour across the four seasons. Winter is a fabulous time to visit the garden—providing of course you can get across the stormy seas. As Andrew sums up, 'that's where we differ very much from mainland gardens; we don't have the winter spell where you have lots of deciduous trees. The garden here is evergreen, there are always over 200 different species in flower...we still have the camellias and that sort of thing, but interspersed with proteas and aloes all coming into flower at the same time—and it all looks just a little bit bizarre. It's more akin to your Mediterranean garden than it would be to a UK garden.'

It certainly it doesn't feel anything like the archetypical English country garden; it is instead a world tour with plants from over 80 countries—without ever appearing artificial. When surrounded by so much exoticism, it's easy to think of the garden as just an intriguing experiment, or even an ecologically unsound folly. The Victorian horticultural era was marked, for example, by numerous attempts to grow anything and everything—however unlikely—on English soil. Huge resources were spent as gardens struggled to outdo each other. Tresco Abbey, however, is a living, breathing entity. The gardeners' expertise is used to place plants where they have the most chance of surviving, but once situated they must thrive, or not, on their own merits. Andrew explains,

'we have quite a few different zones in the garden which are basically down to the soil types and shade. We have four terraces, the top two being hot and dry but also being in the wind; the soil types at the very top of the garden are just peat for two feet maximum with granite underneath—so it's quite poor soil, and can dry out incredibly in the summer.' Nevertheless, these conditions are ideal for South African and Australian plants such as proteas, banksias and callistemons. In contrast, the better soil in the lower garden suits tree ferns and New Zealand plants which are not particularly water retentive. Picking the right location is all important; the garden has no irrigation system and nothing, with the exception of plants in pots or containers, is ever watered.

As well as its unusual plants and trees, the garden also has a rather unusual range of wildlife. Strangely, as Andrew confirms, there are no snakes, frogs, toads, newts, squirrels, badgers or foxes at Tresco Abbey. Instead, there are a multitude of birds of the type frequently seen in mainland gardens—however, what's fun about them is how uncommonly tame they all seem to be. Birds such as goldfinches, greenfinches, sparrows, blackbirds and chaffinches will eat out of your hand or merrily bathe in the fantastic agave-shaped fountain (very fitting in this setting and a nice change from the usual boring old water features) right in front of you. Several pheasants also wander fairly aimlessly around the garden paying scant regard to visitors awed by a close-up view of their splendid plumage. Rather nonchalantly they park themselves on the balustrades and watch the world go by.

The garden is also, to nick a phrase from comedian and executive transvestite Eddie Izzard, covered in bees! Well, not literally, but the addition of five hives at the garden does provide for plenty of bee action—and it's amusing to watch them wiggle their furry behinds whilst working away on a flower. The honey they produce is pretty special too as

"...in the bamboos, tree ferns, palms and fine foliages, it is a man of poor imagination who cannot see the gibbons swinging through the tall trees."
Tom Dorrien-Smith, taken from a lecture given at The Royal Horticultural Society

Andrew notes, 'we usually get over 300 pounds of honey and most of that would go to the abbey, but any spare would go to the garden shop and be sold as probably the most expensive honey anywhere in the UK...it's exclusive because of the range of plants that the bees are feeding off, it tastes completely different but it is also limited edition—first come, first served.' The bees can gather nectar from a plethora of exotic plants flowering throughout the year, meaning they have a longer working season—but they don't seem to be complaining. One bee favourite is the New Zealand Christmas tree—known to the Maoris as the Pohutukawa. These spectacular trees are 60 feet high and have red bottlebrush-shaped flowers covering their canopies, and according to Andrew, are 'absolutely overflowing with nectar'. At their peak in June to July, these massive trees are not to be missed; a vivid burst of colour—heavenly for both visitor and bee.

The birds and the bees accentuate the sense that Tresco is the epitome of the Garden of Eden. However, there is trouble in paradise. The garden's Valhalla Museum is a monument to disaster, filled as it is with the figureheads of ships which have challenged the merciless storms of the Atlantic and lost. The history of shipwrecks is highly significant to the garden—originally many of its exotic plants had to be brought over by ship. Certainly the likes of Augustus Smith and his successors owed a debt to the courage of ship farers. Although temperatures on Tresco are mild—rarely higher than 25 °C in the summer and commonly no lower than 5 °C in the winter— the forces of nature can, and have been, perilous for the garden.

In 1987, the garden faced its worst weather conditions in its 160-year history. Most people remember 1987 as the year of the hurricane, and the garden did receive a battering from the tail end of these strong winds. Some damage did occur, however much worse was to come. Snow rarely settles on Tresco, but that winter the garden was covered in a foot of snow for five days. Andrew recalls, 'we lost about 70 per cent of the garden—all the protea collection, all the aloe collection, some 60-foot-high banksias, Norfolk Island pines of the same sort of size ...Things like aloes [that have] water in the foliage are going to freeze up straight away and just disintegrate.'

Nineteen ninety was another devastating year for the Tresco Abbey, with winds gusting to 128 miles an hour causing the destruction, in just one night, of the majority of the garden's mature 150-year-old shelter belt. Luckily, the twelve month growing season at the garden has allowed trees planted in 1992 to reach heights of 40 feet already.

The future for a garden like this might always seem uncertain, especially with the threat of climate change on the horizon. Twenty eight miles from Land's End and warmed by the Gulf Stream yet blasted by Atlantic gales, there is a feeling of ingenuity about this garden which is almost magical. The Isles of Scilly have mythical associations, and you can see why when visiting this garden—an outpost of abundance and diversity in a landscape of desolate, if beautiful, moorland. Tresco Abbey's sculpture, by David Wynne, represents the garden's debt to the powers of the natural world—Gaia, the earth mother, carved from marble striated in tones of grey and brown, colours which seem to change depending on the light.

A voluptuous symbol of fertility, let's hope she looks after the future of this breathtaking garden. If not, maybe the sacrifice of the odd visitor might suffice. The Puya (for more info, see right) is quite partial to sheep, I'm sure it would settle for a small and tasty child.

The Puya

The Puya, when in flower seemingly a hellish union betwixt triffid and lollipop, is one of Tresco's more bizarre residents. Hailing from Chile, where it can be found growing on the lower slopes of the Andes, this is a plant with a few tricks up its sleeve. Tresco's Puya, planted in 1843, was one of the very first introductions to the garden.

The Puya has since spread out to form an extensive clump commanding an impressive site 60 feet across. In the spring this bromeliad, with a rosette of spiky leaves four feet wide at its base, sends up nine-foot-high, club-like structures with spikes sticking out from the side. From mid April to mid June, two-inch waxy flowers open in vivid shades of chartreuse (*Puya chilensis*) and metallic turquoise (*Puya berteroniana*). The spikes act as perches for starlings and blackbirds who dip into the flowers for nectar, coating their heads with yellow pollen in the process. It's an amazing sight; the makeover really suits these ordinary garden birds which are transformed into birds of paradise. At least that's probably what they tell each other. They remind me of my little sister who still can't eat mashed potato without getting it in her hair.

In its homeland, the Puya has a more malevolent side. Occasionally a sheep grazes too close to the fiendish plant, its woolly fleece becoming entangled on the sharp spikes. Good for the Puya, the animal provides fertiliser; bad for the sheep, which will perish of starvation. At Tresco Abbey, the Puya only has the opportunity to assault the gardeners— none of whom to date have been marooned on its fearsome thorns. Andrew is taking no chances however, laughing wickedly he explains, 'It's definitely a student weeding area because it's very spiky. It's an initiation for them—full set of oilskins on the hottest day in the year, go and pull the brambles and bracken out of it!'

Perilous Plants

The Protea's feathery fleshiness and the Puya's carnivorous tendencies might be a little unnerving. However, many plants are potentially perilous and, more to the point, highly deceptive—who would have thought something as common and innocuous looking as a buttercup might have a mean streak? I've always thought as a theme a poisoner's garden would be rather fun to create, as well as useful (take heed anyone who intends to criticise these pages!). Here are a few examples of venomous vegetation:

Daffodil

The bulbs of these favourites can be fatal, causing nausea, vomiting and diarrhoea.

Hemlock

Considered a weed, and no wonder, this is not the sort of plant you want to surround yourself with. The filthy killer of Socrates amongst others, all parts of this plant are extremely dangerous—a dose of only 0.15 g would be lethal to adults. If you decide to give it a try expect nausea, vomiting, increasing difficulty with speech and movement, dilation of pupils leading to paralysis of the limbs then paralysis of the thoracic muscles and then…. you feel great! No, not really, instead you get to entertain the Grim Reaper. According to Plato, Socrates coped admirably with his promised extinction, 'his legs became colder and colder, he lay upon the garden-seat and kept talking to the people around. He kept his thoughts and mind clear till the very end.'

Lily of the Valley

The leaves and the flowers of the pretty plant cause

an irregular heart beat and pulse which are frequently accompanied by digestive upset and mental confusion.

Rhododendron

If you had just munched on some Lily of the Valley and were feeling a tad mentally confused, you might chomp on these as well. Along with azaleas, rhododendrons are not just a nightmare to spell but can be fatal. The ingestion of any part of the plant can result in nausea, vomiting, depression, difficulty breathing, and coma.

Highlights

The Plants

An unusual one for me in my capacity as horticulturally challenged, but the plant range will not fail to impress: The strange Puya, the King Protea (national flower of South Africa); the ubiquitous *Aeonium*; the *Leucadendron argenteum* or silver tree, its distinct silvery tone created by dense hairs covering its foliage; the lively profusion of colour created by abundant *Osteospermum* and *Senecio* species and the shimmering flowers of the *Lampranthus* succulent; and the simply huge examples of agave. Each is a highlight on its own, but when viewed together, within the context of the garden, the result is unforgettable.

Island Paradise

The Isles of Scilly (pronounced 'silly') are made up of 140 islands, only 6 of which are inhabited. The Scilly Isles defiantly have their own identity, distinct even to that of Cornwall—natural perhaps in a location so remote which, in winter, can be bleak. History and myth are deeply ingrained in the culture of the Scillies—legend says that Tresco is 'Lyonesse' or 'land across the sea', the final resting place of King Arthur.

Home to the Abbey Garden, Tresco is the second largest of the islands with fantastic scenery, from rugged heathland strewn with granite outcrops to glorious sandy beaches. No cars are permitted on the island making it a peaceful idyll. With clear blue skies, and swathes of statuesque *Agapanthus* on the sea shores in the summer months, Tresco truly doesn't feel like part of the UK. It has an unspoilt beauty that can hold its own against anywhere in the world and makes an exotic venue for Tresco Abbey, the most exotic of gardens.

Sweet Honey

Well I'd imagine this to be a highlight, but it is so bloomin' exclusive that it was sold out when I last visited the garden! Be wise and get there early.

The Abbey Garden, Tresco, Isles of Scilly, Cornwall, TR24 0QQ, 01720 424105
www.tresco.co.uk

TREBAH GARDENS

Nr Falmouth, Cornwall

Coastal   Jungle   Inclusive   Heroic   Outlandish

Head gardener Darren Dickey believes that Trebah is special for visitors and resident gardeners alike because, 'it feels all part of one; it doesn't feel like it's divided into lots of little gardens from different parts of the world—although it is a mixture of planting from all the four corners of the globe. It feels like you've just sort of clambered up the mountainside into the Himalayan undergrowth; it really does have a magic feel about it.' Darren clearly loves his job and was motivated to seek a career in horticulture from a very young age—as a child he enjoyed working in his grandfather's vegetable plot. He believes that people often don't appreciate how 'therapeutic' gardens can be, 'We've had quite a few volunteers, students and career changers who have come to work at Trebah, and they've grown to realise in the time that they've been here just how inspiring it can be to be part of creating something.' Darren has been at Trebah for nearly fifteen years, so has had the opportunity to see the garden evolve, to see trees mature, and witness the effects of his own, and his team's, work. This, he tells us, is part of the reason he finds gardening so satisfying.

Trebah is certainly a garden that has seen plenty of change since it was first acquired in 1831 by the meticulous Quaker, Charles Fox. Each tree had to be positioned perfectly and Fox would instruct his head gardener to erect a scaffold tower representing the height the tree would be expected to reach. An unfortunate garden boy would then be sent up the rickety tower with a white flag, which he was ordered to wave when he reached the top. With the aid of a megaphone and a telescope, Fox would look out for the flag from his attic window, shouting orders and often demanding the tower was moved and rebuilt until he was happy with the location for the tree. Considering trees take so long to mature, forward thinking was obviously one of Fox's qualities.

Charles Fox's daughter married into the Backhouse family and in the next thirty years Trebah became less concerned with trees (originally it was created as a pinetum and it was Fox who designed the shelter belt which encircles and protects the garden today), and instead acquired a world famous collection of rare and exotic plants.

In 1907, the garden was bought by Charles Hawkins Hext, and his wife Alice, who threw themselves into its further development introducing many varieties of tender plants including bamboos. After Alice's death in 1939, however, the garden was largely neglected until Tony and Eira Hibbert purchased Trebah in 1980.

Kids Play

Head gardener Darren learnt his trade via a Youth Training Scheme apprenticeship, and believes horticulture is, 'a great way of life, it's personal satisfaction.' Why not attempt to get children interested in gardens and gardening? Maybe like Darren, they'll love it so much they'll make a career of it, rather than working in telesales and living for a weekend fuelled by binge drinking—not that I'm knocking binge drinking, obviously. Anyway, a few ideas:

Sunflowers

The ideal plant for a child as they're easy and quick to grow, sprouting in just one week. Children can compete to see whose flower reaches the most impressive height, and the seeds can be roasted for snacks rich in iron or used as bird feed. Plus, sunflowers attract a bountiful amount of insects, which can encourage a child's interest in the natural world. Indeed, bees love sunflowers so much they don't even care if they're real! Researchers at the University of London placed paintings under bee flight paths and found that they approached and landed most frequently on floral artwork—unsurprisingly, Van Gogh's 'Sunflowers' was the favourite.

Bed time

Whether this is a raised bed, a ground plot or even just a garden container, give children the opportunity to have their own small area in which to grow plants. Don't be mean, give them a location with the best soil and light so they are not discouraged by too many planting failures. Let them choose what they want to grow (but point them in the direction of fast growing, manageable plants) and get them to draw a picture of what they want their plot to look like.

Realising the significance of Trebah as a garden that encompasses the visions and ideas of its successive owners, the Hibbert family gave the estate to The Trebah Garden Trust, a registered charity that will ensure the garden's preservation for future generations to enjoy.

Trebah, pronounced Tree-ba to clear up any confusion, is Celtic for 'house on the bay', but has become synonymous with everything that makes Cornish gardens so admired worldwide. As a Cornish girl myself, I'm well used to the rain; in fact I blame my insufficient height on the constant pelting of rain on my head—I mean, how was I supposed to grow against that? Fortunately the gardens of Cornwall thrive on the mild, wet conditions. This uniquely miserable

weather (although it *is* lovely in summer—it was on a Wednesday last year I seem to remember...) means that an array of exotic and temperate plants and trees positively flourish here. And Trebah is the perfect example—a real sub-tropical jungle of a garden.

The almost tangible sense of excitement at Trebah begins at the Visitor Centre, which (smart as it is) might as well be a magical wardrobe: walking through the door is like discovering another world, or at least a new country. And all for a very reasonable admission price too and no polluting air travel necessary (unless you're not a UK citizen, in which case, yay, I've broken the foreign market!). Throw in a private secluded beach to laze about on when you're

bored of 'oohing' and 'ahhing' over matters botanical, and it's easy to ask: what more could you want? How many gardens do you think can provide you with that?

Well, Trebah can. Spending the summer in gardens could not be described as a hardship, but research at Trebah was all the more enlightening for this writer—nothing like a swim in clean blue waters to sharpen the mind.

A near tragedy, then, for the world of horticulture as well as my own personal enjoyment, that these gardens were virtually lost forever. When Major Tony Hibbert and his wife Eira bought Trebah they were hoping for a home with 'no work, no worries and no responsibilities where we could eek out our last remaining days of retirement in peace and quiet.' Then aged 62, the Major's ultimate plan after purchasing Trebah was, 'to sit on the terrace every morning in the sun drinking gin and going down to the private beach every afternoon to launch our little dinghy and sail and fish every afternoon.' Well that all sounds very pleasant, although gin in the morning is perhaps a tad hardcore. But obviously not for the Major, who after all is a decorated Paratrooper and veteran of Dunkirk and Arnhem—for Tony there is probably no such thing as a 'gin too far'.

The plan worked perfectly for the first week, but on the Sunday the Secretary of the Cornwall Garden Society, Dr Challinor C. Davies, popped round to spoil the bliss. After yet more gin he showed the Hibberts that 'underneath the jungle which had grown up in the last 42 years there was the remains of this very, very important and very beautiful garden.' By the time the bottle had been drained, and presumably the company were completely sloshed, he had convinced the couple to restore the grounds telling them, 'you have here one of the most beautiful gardens in England and horticulturally one of the most important; if you leave it, and do nothing about it, it will be lost forever…so I leave it to your conscience…if you devote the next 3 years to restoring the garden you will have done yourselves and horticulture a great service.' Well after that guilt trip, what could they do?

So, with no experience of gardening whatsoever, Tony, Eira and a friend, ex SAS sergeant Carol Chin, armed themselves with machetes and entered the fray. They soon realised that the friendly Garden Society Secretary, whilst keen to sample the delights of the Hibbert drinks cabinet, had 'lied through his teeth'. The restoration of Trebah was never likely to be finished in a mere three years, rather it has become a labour of love keeping the Hibberts busy for more than 25 years.

The couple have an abundance of anecdotes about the garden, a favourite being a story relating the visit of Edward VIII, who was then Prince of Wales, and Wallis Simpson in 1934. They were shown round the garden, finishing in the banana grove (which is now the koi carp pond). The Major continues, 'the Prince of Wales was enormously impressed. All the banana trees, which were about four or five metres high, had huge bunches of ripe edible

Trebah is described as the 'garden of dreams', but what does dreaming of gardens actually signify? Well, some folklore suggests the meaning is dependent on the type or condition of the garden. Dreaming of a vegetable garden means that prosperity through hard work and discipline will be yours, whilst a flower garden foretells of true love, tranquillity and a happy future. Nightmarish visions of meagre, weed-infested gardens, however, imply a neglect of spiritual needs…and perhaps also a lack of enthusiasm for gardening!

bananas. So the Prince of Wales congratulated the head gardener, said he'd never seen bananas ripening in the open before in England, and he gave him a tip equivalent to today's standards of about £120, which pleased the head gardener no end—until the next morning the head gardener was summoned by the owner of the house and sacked for gross incompetence and impertinence. Because of course the head gardener had been down to Falmouth the day before, bought all the bananas and wired them on very carefully.' A true story with photographs to prove it apparently, and all the more amusing because the gardener wasn't sacked for his deception, but because in his hurry he left a label on one of the bananas!

On a less lighthearted note, Trebah is also famous for its role in the Second World War. In 1944, the beach was covered in concrete and a regiment of 7,500 men from the 29th US Infantry Division embarked from it in order to land on Omaha Beach in Normandy for the D-Day assault. To commemorate the 60th anniversary of the end of WWII and the D-Day landings, the culmination of a year-long project provided art installations and dance performances with the spectacular surroundings of Trebah, and neighbouring garden Glendurgan, as a backdrop. A collaboration between young people from fifteen primary, junior, and secondary schools, colleges, local community groups and professional artists produced a remarkable series of events over the course

of a week—all inspired by Cornwall's participation in the WWII. Some of the art was quirky, some humorous, some much more evocative of the horrors of the battlefield, the fear of losing loved ones and the loneliness of evacuees.

But what seemed apt about Trebah's involvement in the project is that this is a garden that both remembers and records the past whilst looking forward to the future. An inclusive garden which welcomes people of all ages, and especially, in a milieu usually considered the domain of the blue rinse brigade, children. From nature trails to school workshops, and not forgetting the entertainment gained from scampering under the giant rhubarb, there's plenty here to entice the potential gardeners of the future.

Highlights

Monster Leaves

Many gardens have *Gunnera manicata,* but not like Trebah; they have the giantest giant rhubarb around. Take the winding path through the Gunnera Passage where the huge prehistoric-looking leaves of this Brazilian plant tower over you menacingly, their undersides covered in devilish thorns. These plants grow up to 16ft high in summer with leaves 8ft in width—not to be missed!

The Bamboozle

When the bamboo matures to a sufficient size the plants will be used to form a maze—hence the name of this area of the garden. And it shouldn't take too long—what is incredible about these plants is how quickly they grow, in summer months sometimes as much as a foot in just one day! Trebah has a variety of these beautiful Asian grasses— including the unusual black bamboo.

And Finally...the Setting

Gardens have to work with their surroundings and there're very few who wouldn't be jealous of Trebah's stunning situation. The Chilean Comb provides Trebah with its famous view down the ravine to the blue of the sea beyond. In spring, the valley is a haze of colour, bluebells, magnolias, rhododendrons, all a vivid underlay to the drama of the Chusan Palms—themselves the tallest in England. The beach, revealing a typically Cornish seascape, is a total contrast to the exoticism of the garden. It's the perfect place to take some time out for yourself, to think about the more important things in life—and maybe to tell someone you love them. Because Trebah is truly a garden that resonates with history and romance.

It is worth every step that you walk.
Thank you for sharing it.
Johannes and Kathy, South Africa.

EASILY THE BEST GARDEN IN CORNWALL
- BEATS All THE REST FOR ITS BEAUTY AND TRANQUILLITY.
WAY BETTER THAN EDEN !
DAN , SURREY , UK

Fantastic Gardens - thoroughly enjoyed sniffing
every inch!! Thanks so much for letting us 4 legged
one's in x
Jack the Welshie, Wales

no wizards
Luke Falmouth UK

Spectacular gardens, beautifully
maintained, will recommend to all.
Best wishes
Sanjeev Bhaskar & Meera Syal
(The Kumars at No 42)

A marvellous place for walking and dreaming.
lovely Garden

Silke + Liam – Germany.

Outstanding beauty and truly an inspiration.
A total haven! Then when you think you've
Seen it all... you see the beach. Wow!
Auerbach, Manchester, UK

Bloomin' beautiful! Breathtaking, even in the rain!

Jayne and Daniel, Berkshire, UK.

Trebah Gardens, Mawnan Smith, Nr Falmouth, Cornwall, TR11 5JZ, 01326 252200
www.trebahgarden.co.uk

PRIDEAUX PLACE

Padstow, Cornwall

Ancient   Ghostly   Renewal   Atmospheric   Superstitious

The house at Prideaux Place is worlds away from your average two up, two down property—a magnificent building, blending the traditional E-shape of Elizabethan architecture with Gothic exuberance. Vacuuming is surely a nightmare; the house contains eighty-four rooms—forty of which are in severe need of a makeover, having remained untouched since the American army were billeted here during WWII. When Elisabeth and Peter Prideaux-Brune took up residence in 1988, dry rot was just one of the many challenges they faced: crumbling temples, overgrown gardens...oh, and the house's slight infestation of ghosts. So would you really want to live here? Elisabeth Prideaux-Brune's answer is clearly a resounding 'yes!' She describes Prideaux Place as 'the most magic place to live, I can't imagine anywhere more beautiful; you can sit in your bath and see the Camel estuary and the deer roaming in the park—how special is that?' Pretty special by anyone's reckoning, I'd think.

Of course, what distinguishes Prideaux Place from most houses (at least the ones on my street) is its rich history and its sheer age. The Prideaux family have lived in Cornwall for one thousand years (with the exception of a relatively brief sojourn in Devon for 200 years) and are descendants of William the Conqueror, Edward I and Queen Eleanor of Castile. Prideaux Place, itself home to fourteen generations of the family, was built by Sir Nicolas Prideaux, with work starting in 1585 and finishing, as Elizabeth recalls with a smile, 'finally in Cornish fashion, dreckly in 1592.'

There are a plethora of stories about Prideaux Place, including political conspiracies, piracy and even a 'murder' which never was! After so much intrigue, and in such an ancient building, perhaps it is not surprising that the house has a *haunting* reputation. Prideaux has appeared on television's 'Most Haunted' and Elisabeth calmly acknowledges, 'There have been ghosts—I mean I've actually seen a couple myself, a lot of people feel there's a presence in the house sometimes. I've got a little kitchen boy who runs in the pantry but he's not remotely frightening—I've seen him two or three times. Before we were married, the classic lady in white walked through the bedroom and into the bathroom. I just assumed she was one of the ancestors checking me out!'

Perhaps the ghosts are a happy bunch because they live in such a happy place—what's really nice about Prideaux is that it isn't a mere timepiece, but a real family home. This is something the public definitely relate to, 'The whole place has a very special feeling about it; lots of people mention how the atmosphere in the house is very warm, it's not a daunting house.' Prideaux Place is also a popular venue for filming—it has been used for more adaptations of Rosamunde Pilcher novels than anywhere else, and has provided the backdrop to an array of films including 'Twelfth Night' with Helena Bonham Carter and Ben Kingsley, and 'Oscar and Lucinda' with Ralph Fiennes and Cate Blanchett.

When not hobnobbing with the stars, Elisabeth is busy with the restoration of Prideaux's grounds. She tells us, 'You can't imagine a house like this without a garden,' but sadly, as with many great houses, the gardens fell into disrepair during WWII. Work began only five years ago to re-establish the lost gardens of Prideaux; nevertheless, in Elisabeth's words, 'the bones are here and, in my opinion, there're no finer views anywhere in the county. It is a garden of vistas.' Prideaux Place has certainly had a thrilling past, and with the continuing evolution of the gardens, it looks like the future will be just as compelling.

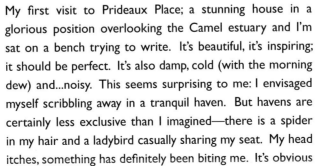

My first visit to Prideaux Place; a stunning house in a glorious position overlooking the Camel estuary and I'm sat on a bench trying to write. It's beautiful, it's inspiring; it should be perfect. It's also damp, cold (with the morning dew) and...noisy. This seems surprising to me: I envisaged myself scribbling away in a tranquil haven. But havens are certainly less exclusive than I imagined—there is a spider in my hair and a ladybird casually sharing my seat. My head itches, something has definitely been biting me. It's obvious

then that Prideaux Place is alive with something more than just history...and also that I've lived in a town too long. It's no wonder that the grounds are home to so much wildlife, as the Prideaux-Brunes believe in keeping the place as naturalistic and in balance with the surroundings as possible. This is reflected in the woodland walks where wild garlic, considered by many to be an over-zealous weed, is allowed to run riot, investing the area with its distinctive scent. The gardens at Prideaux Place are certainly not the epitome of

pristine perfection, where the natural environment has been beaten into submission. However, this was not always the case.

It appears to have been Edmund Prideaux who first showed an interest in the gardens; his drawings from the 1730s reveal the landscaping and hedged walks he was to add. Typically for the era, Edmund had a love of renaissance art gained from his Grand Tour experiences—this influence manifests itself via a scattering of Roman-influenced buildings across his grounds such as a classically styled temple, an obelisk, a grotto and an exedra which is home to funerary urns dating all the way back to 50 AD. His son Humphrey, possibly thinking it a tad bizarre to have Roman relics in a Cornish garden, and wanting to move with the times, redesigned the grounds in a more naturalistic 'Capability Brown' fashion. In 1870, the addition of a sunken garden with a quatrefoil design brought some formality to the grounds.

A photograph from 1902 shows this Georgian-style garden to be immaculately planted; no surprise when you consider that 12-14 gardeners were employed at this time. I can't imagine there was a place for disorder in those early days, no ladybirds lounging on benches, no wildflowers littering the lawns. Colonel Charles Prideaux–Brune was particularly enamoured of the formal garden and loved to show it off to his guests. A story describes how he would bring out a group to admire its splendour in the morning before church. On his return, he would again request that his friends (who probably considered him delusional) admire the gardens; when they did so, they were greeted with a completely different vision. In the short time between visits, Charles had ordered his gardeners to replant the whole of the sunken garden (they must have loved him, and his wonderful sense of humour!).

What this little tale demonstrates so well, is how gardens and gardening have changed since Edwardian and Victorian times. No one can afford to employ a whole troop of

gardeners these days, and often gardens need to be adapted so they are no longer so high maintenance. This is certainly the case here, where the gardens have suffered neglect in recent times.

Excitingly, however, this is a new era for Prideaux. With the assistance of Tom Petherick, instrumental in the restoration of the Lost Gardens of Heligan, the grounds are being regenerated. Tom explains that the gardens have been redesigned 'along the lines of how it might have been in times gone by' but also to be in keeping with their location. 'It is very much a woodland garden, so we've gone for the type of woodland plants you see throughout Cornwall in gardens of this nature...camellias, one or two big Asiatic magnolias, rhododendrons, but also an underlay of more herbaceous shrubs...we've got echiums, hydrangeas—things that are very much of the county.' Pernicious species of plants such as laurel and sycamore had taken over and needed clearing, whilst some parts of the gardens were so overgrown that they had to be traced with the help of an ordinance survey map and a piece of string! A massive amount of work has been necessary to restore the gardens to their former glory, and yet more is underway—a recent addition is the Lime Avenue. Nevertheless, it is obvious how worthwhile an experience it has been for everyone involved. Tom, who has had 'great fun' working at Prideaux, describes why he feels it's such a unique place: 'I think the layout, the situation of the house and the lands around it are really very special. It's been here such a long time...the atmosphere around here is a very ancient one, filled with history and you can feel the aged quality it has—you can hear the building talk.'

The fallow deer at Prideaux Place are a scatty bunch—getting close enough to photograph them was quite a task. Heads raised, they all glare at you suspiciously, obviously assuming you're about to mug them and steal their belongings. No chance of that; as soon as you've edged to a distance where you just about make out their lovely white spots, they are away, in full flight, graceful and free, covering the ground at an amazing speed. I had expected that deer kept in a park would be somewhat tame; after all, I've had wild deer approach me and allow me to stroke their velvety heads. But these guys are seriously paranoid—I expect they even worry about the threat of terrorism. However, there's something reassuring about their sheer inimical wildness, something truly beautiful. As a child I remember petting a couple of deer at a park somewhere, to be later informed that the park was actually a venison farm. I think I'd seen Bambi fairly recently, so obviously I was upset—but it seemed all the more disturbing to me that the animals would go meekly and compliantly to their deaths, believing humans their protectors and possibly even friends. So the deer are right to be wary; just bring your binoculars if you're visiting.

The deer park is thought to be the oldest in the country—it has been dated back to its Roman enclosure in 435 AD—and its history is intrinsically bound up with the Prideaux story. According to legend, the continued existence of the family rests on the survival of the deer. When the Prideaux clan's bloodline was declining, a worried King George V dispatched a virile young buck via train to Padstow from his Windsor herd. Promptly, the next morning, the poor deer was shot—the gamekeeper had set out to cull the old lead buck and got the wrong one. An unfortunate mistake, or perhaps the gamekeeper didn't particularly like his employers, but the Prideaux-Brunes seem none the worse for it. Bet the buck wished he'd missed that train though.

Highlights

Before and After

Just like one of those TV makeover shows...only slower. It's been a revelation to see the transformation of the gardens. Yes admittedly, the plants take their time, but this already unique and stunning attraction is just going to get better and better.

'Obby 'Oss Day

'Obby 'Oss Day in Padstow is that well-known phenomenon—the strange Cornish custom. It's great fun! It starts early in the morning with the sacrifice of thirteen specially picked, irritating tourists (locally known as emmets) then...oops, wrong one. This is actually a festival held every year on the 1st of May to celebrate spring and fertility; its origins are blatantly pagan. Revellers throng the streets of the picturesque fishing village and a procession moves to the beat of drums, finally ending up at Prideaux Place itself. A good time is had by all, dancing, drinking...and, if you're female, trying to avoid being dragged under the cloak of hobby horses with big red eyes and snapping teeth. If you get assaulted by one of these two quite bizarre apparitions, it could make you fertile, so remember to take protection.

The Bluebell (*Hyacinthoides non-scripta*)

With its woodland areas, Prideaux is a great place to see bluebells. In a recent poll, this flower was voted the nation's favourite and it's easy to see why. Dazzling with a sea of blue when growing en masse, bluebells give woodlands an air of mystery and enchantment. However, despite their apparent abundance, they are, according to conservationists, under threat both from theft of bulbs from natural woodland areas and from the larger Spanish variety with which they hybridise freely. So probably best to leave them alone, especially as they appear to have a dark side. Tradition associates the bluebell with the Hyacinth of the ancients, the flower of grief and mourning. Folklore also suggests that if you hear a bluebell ring, then death awaits you. The bluebell is the flower that will alert fairies to your presence in their habitat—and we're not talking about Tinkerbell, these guys are nasty. It's understandable really; after all, it is illegal to pick native wildflowers.

Prideaux Place, Padstow, Cornwall, PL28 8RP, 01841 532411
www.prideauxplace.co.uk

PENCARROW

Nr Bodmin, Cornwall

Historic   Freeing   Playful   Leisurely   Welcoming

'Originally it was two giraffes looking through the roof, then one fell down in a gale,' laughs Lady Molesworth-St Aubyn, sitting outside her kitchen at Pencarrow House, 'and then the roof fell down! Life's never dull here you know!' This is a story that needs some explaining; Pencarrow is home to plenty of wildlife, as well as an array of chickens and strutting peacocks—but, as yet, no giraffes. However, the huge palm with its trunk stretching far above the tumbled-down remains of what was once a Palm House does indeed bear a passing resemblance to the aforementioned long-necked creature. The Palm House is certainly unconventional, but seems indicative of the playful attitude that reigns at Pencarrow, along with a stoic ability to cope with whatever challenges life brings.

It is perhaps facile to assume that anyone possessing such a massive estate must automatically have the means to care for it. But Lady Molesworth-St Aubyn explains that it's 'a real struggle' and makes the point that even simple-sounding jobs can be tricky at Pencarrow: 'For instance today, putting on the lights in the front hall for a coach party; one of the lights wouldn't work so we changed the bulb, shook the light, kicked the light—it won't work. It's old.'

The house had been standing empty for 18 years when Lady Molesworth-St Aubyn first took up residence with her husband and family. The roof was leaky, complete rewiring was required and the gardens were pretty much overgrown. She recalls, 'and it was utterly miserable—big houses need people basically.' Restoring the estate has had to be a gradual process because of the massive expense involved, and there are still plenty of projects left to do. Luckily, Pencarrow's natural charm has encouraged people to pitch in, 'We've got a marvellous group of people called Friends of Pencarrow, who have been an enormous help. It's so wonderful to have somebody else who's actually interested, somebody outside the family who wants Pencarrow to go on.'

The gardens have had to move with the times, and they can no longer be maintained at such a high standard. As Lady Molesworth-St Aubyn admits, 'The Italian Garden isn't as it ought to be, it's been simplified. All the beds were got rid of, and I believe my mother-in-law had her favourite bull calf grazing the lawn—it ended up in the fountain one day!' Wildflowers are now encouraged, adding to the relaxed, naturalistic feel of the garden. Lady Molesworth-St Aubyn obviously approves, 'I think it's nice because dogs and children can run around, they don't have to stick to any paths, and there are lots of secret places that children can go and hide... it's rather different than normal gardens, there's lots of space.' There's such a pleasant atmosphere at Pencarrow; a garden that has had to adapt, but is all the better for it.

Bright sunshine greeted me on my first visit to Pencarrow; my second ended in drunken dishevelment—but more of that later. It was obvious from the first that Pencarrow was not simply a horticulturist's playground, but a unique opportunity for the public to enjoy a gorgeous country estate in a variety of ways.

Pencarrow and its gardens are imbued with history. The Molesworth family and their descendants the Molesworth-St Aubyns have owned the estate since the reign of Queen Elizabeth I. They seem to be related to absolutely all the landed gentry in Cornwall—the house is chock full of portraits of baronets and their wives, and as far as I'm concerned confusion reigns. Take a tour of the house if you need to know more, as I'm lost in a thick smog of aristocratic names and titles, royal associations, and tales of illegitimacy. It is clear however, that they were a busy bunch; fourth Baronet Sir John Molesworth, for instance, founded a banking house which shared his name. Eventually that company became Lloyds Bank and was never to be heard of again (yep, I'm lying).

The Grade II listed historical gardens at Pencarrow were the brainchild of radical statesman Sir William Molesworth (he was the eighth Baronet for those of you counting). Work commenced with the elegant sunken Italian Garden, which perfectly complements the square formal design of the Georgian-style house that it accompanies. The Rock Garden, which is the first of its kind, predating even that of Chatsworth, was built using granite from Bodmin Moor.

Sir William allegedly oversaw the placing of every single stone, which were transported to the garden with the help of his tenants—grateful for his assistance during the difficult period before the repeal of the Corn Laws. An ancient Cornish Cross (which apparently was just 'found' in a field somewhere) also adorns the area.

In 1842, he began the ambitious project of the mile-long carriage drive, ensuring that it was lined with specimen conifers obtained from all the great botanical explorers of the age. (In fact, famous plant hunters William and Thomas Lobb were actually born on the estate—yet another indicator of Pencarrow's horticultural historical significance).

It seems that Sir William was a true visionary. In his political career, he fought for reform and was responsible for abolishing the transportation of prisoners to Australia—it's always refreshing to come across historical figures who sound like decent people, it makes me like his garden all the more.

Perhaps it is also the case that it takes a visionary character to create a great garden; it is so hard to visualise the results of planned endeavours. William, however, was as successful at garden design as he was at politics. His energy and enthusiasm for the gardens allowed him to contend, shortly before his death in 1855, that he had planted every known conifer (except ten) hardy enough to survive in the British climate.

The garden continued to evolve after his death, with significant additions being the Bog Garden planted in memory of Lt Col Sir Arscott Molesworth-St Aubyn (the fifteenth Baronet). Overcoming his mouthful of a name, Sir Arscott had a career with the Royal Green Jackets and also inherited a love of the gardens. He worked to restore the gardens to their former glory after they had been left derelict during WW2.

Although in many respects the gardens at Pencarrow still resemble Sir William's original designs, modern attitudes and concerns now prevail. The Rock Garden cost the eighth Baronet £20,000 to build—a huge amount of money back in the 1800s. Nowadays, these estates are so expensive to maintain that money is always a problem. Victorian gardening was often concerned with achieving the near impossible; about showing off, it seems. For instance, a chronicle of the era contains an article about a Pencarrow head gardener's pride at growing a Venus Flytrap all winter in the Rock Garden. Now, however, plants are chosen for their suitability to the garden's conditions, both for economic and environmental reasons. Gavin, Pencarrow's amiable head gardener, notes that in Victorian gardens 'everything had to conform.' He laughs when asked what Sir William would think of the gardens at present: 'He'd sack all the gardeners that are here today for sure!'

But Pencarrow actually benefits from the loosening of discipline. Areas of long grass, where wildflowers flourish, are now actively encouraged, providing habitats for wildlife. And, perhaps what Sir William might find most surprising, his Italian lawns and woodland trails are now open to the public—what would he think of concerts in the meadow and children rolling on the grass? Well, unfortunately for him he's far too dead for his potential answers to be taken seriously. For me, its Pencarrow's relaxed, unfussed atmosphere that makes it such a pleasurable place to visit.

A curious aspect of Cornwall (and England as a whole) is that although it is relatively easy to find yourself surrounded by countryside and glorious landscapes, it is often a case of look but don't touch. It is increasingly difficult to find off-road places where dogs can run free or a picnic can be enjoyed. For this reason places such as Pencarrow should be truly valued. There are no pedantic 'keep off the grass' signs here and no misers to shout at children doing what children love to do best (creating havoc, noisily.) A popular venue for weddings (the head gardener recently found a wedding guest the morning after the big day, fast asleep on the lawn), and with a varied programme of events, there's a reason for just about anyone to find some fun at Pencarrow—kids are catered for with musical and circus theme days, to name a few. On my very first visit to Pencarrow, a Red Setter in fantastic condition bolted past me along the woodland walk, jumping in and out of the stream in the Bog Garden, and I came to the quick conclusion that the estate is a pooch paradise. So it's no surprise that the garden was the winner of the Dog Trust's 'Attraction of the Year' in 2004 (voted for by dogs, probably).

Of course, all the walking your dog will hassle you to do is likely to be exhausting; in which case the best options are a snooze on the grass, a Cornish cream tea in the Tearooms or a picnic. If you decide on the latter, stop on at the nearby Camel Valley Vineyard which produces lovely wine ideal for sipping on a sunny day. Believe me, I know, having tried most of their varieties and ending up in a somewhat disordered state (it was sunstroke, I'm sure of it). Luckily, heightened states of mind and a certain amount of drunkenness are expected from a writer, as obviously inspiration is everything, and that's just what you'll find at Pencarrow.

Strawberry Smoothie

Ingredients

1 punnet of fresh Pencarrow strawberries
½ tsp of vanilla extract
1½ cups of low fat vanilla yoghurt or natural yoghurt,
Greek yoghurt or vanilla ice cream
400 ml apple juice
Handful of crushed ice (optional)

Serves 4—depending on thirst levels!

Wash strawberries, remove their stalks.

Add your choice of yoghurt or ice cream to blender with one quarter of the apple juice. Switch on, then throw in strawberries and ice if required; blend until smooth. Finish by adding the remaining apple juice, add less if you want a really thick smoothie, and blend on full power until thoroughly smooth. Serve immediately.

The low fat yoghurt is a healthy alternative, Greek yoghurt will give a creamier taste and the ice cream is ideal for when you need to indulge! If it's a boiling hot day, add ice for a frosty, cooling drink.

Strawberries are full of vitamins C and A, plus a good source of minerals such as potassium and calcium. This is a delicious, healthy way to enjoy strawberries picked in Pencarrow's garden!

Gooseberry Fool

Ingredients

600 g Pencarrow gooseberries
180 g Greek yoghurt or double cream
100 g golden caster sugar

Serves 4

Preheat oven to gas mark 4, 350 °F (180 °C). Place gooseberries in a shallow baking tray and sprinkle on sugar.

Bake on the centre shelf for 20-30 minutes, or until tender when tested. When baked, sieve away excess juice into a bowl and save.

Next add three quarters of the gooseberries to a blender, add 4 tbsp of the juice and blend to a thick puree.

Leave puree until it is cold, empty yoghurt into a bowl, stir then add half the puree.

Add mixture to glasses, spooning the remaining puree on to the top and garnish with the remaining gooseberries. Cover and chill before serving.

This is a really simple recipe allowing the full flavour of the gooseberries to be appreciated. Pick some tart, juicy gooseberries at the garden—packed with vitamins A and C, full of fibre, this undervalued fruit can be used in an array of tempting recipes.

Highlights

The Drive

This mile-long carriage drive to the house was created to make an impression, and in the spring with an abundance of colour provided by rhododendrons and azaleas it does just that. But it won't work its magic if you whiz down it in your car. To really appreciate it you should get out and walk, at least part of the way (clippity clop noises and proceeding at a collected trot is also an option—and is advised as amusing other visitors will make you popular...).

Pick Your Own Fruit

Perfect for an impromptu picnic on a glorious summer's day. See recipes either side for ideas of what else to do with it!

Pencarrow, Washaway, Bodmin, Cornwall, PL30 3AG, 01208 841369
www.pencarrow.co.uk

DOCTON MILL GARDENS

Hartland Peninsula, Devon

Green   Lifestyle   Natural   Tranquil   Water

John Borrett describes the purchase of Docton Mill Gardens as 'the worst property deal I've ever been involved in'. He goes on to explain that he and his wife Lana were 'so, so besotted, it meant so much to us, in the fact that it would be a lifestyle change, we were both getting out of careers that we didn't like...when at 11am on Friday the 17th of March we were told the money had gone through, and we could move into the house—well I had a grin that went from ear to ear.'

John worked as a mechanical engineer, and as Lana explains, the monotony didn't exactly suit him, 'Stuck behind a computer for ten hours a day...he detested it, absolutely hated it.' Skiving off from his oppressive employment—because he was basically fed up at work and wanted a day off—gave him his first glimpse of Docton Mill Gardens. What he saw that day was to radically change his life; he felt instantly that the gardens were 'magical', describing them as 'mind-blowing' and saying that as soon as he reached the entrance he was 'working out sums in my head.'

The couple now run Docton Mill Gardens together, and I get the distinct impression that Lana is the linchpin, working tirelessly to provide visitors with refreshments, whilst John revels in the freedom of working outside in his wellies. Lana had previously worked with people that had learning disabilities, 'great people, great staff—but long, challenging hours.' The change of pace seems to have been opportune for the pair's relationship too. Amazingly, people seem to really open up on camera, and in an interview John hints that Lana and he had 'tremendous' difficulties in the past, but now describes their marriage as 'very strong.' The stress of modern life taking its toil has almost become a cliché—no doubt because it is often the case—but for John and Lana getting back to nature seems to have really done the trick.

A modern fairytale then, and with an increasingly old-fashioned happy ending. Except it is no ending. The Borretts didn't just purchase a dream; they have made the dream work for them. Regarding gardening credentials, John searches for the word to describe his horticultural knowledge and finally settles on 'zero.' Nevertheless, it didn't stop the Docton Mill Gardens team from winning a gold medal at the Devon County Show in, what's needless to say, was their first attempt at designing and building a show garden.

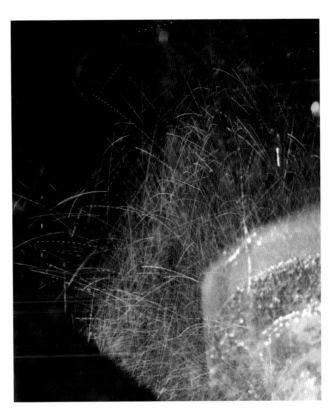

Okay, okay, so John and Lana *did* have some assistance with their venture. Although no longer at Docton Mill, gardener Sarah Harket worked at the gardens for many years. Her horticultural values have helped to make the gardens special. Sarah's background and training is in organic gardening, and she likes to keep everything as naturalistic as possible. This was certainly reflected in her design for the county show, where there was hardly any brown soil to be seen amongst the lush, vibrant profusion of plants. Her idea was to take Docton Mill to the show, 'we wanted to give a feel of different parts of the garden...basically we picked up bits of Docton and crammed it into a small space.'

There were moments of panic, however, when some potential stars of the show just weren't ready for their close-ups, 'there were a few plants which just sat in their pots and did nothing.' Luckily the candelabra *Primula* and the Hortensia (hydrangea), with its big purple flowers, performed beautifully, as did the Amber Angel Kiss (a very pretty type of pansy) and a large viburnum tree that caused some difficulty in transportation but, as Sarah notes, added 'real strength of character' to the show garden.

John clearly loved the experience and, maybe a little embarrassingly for himself, was quite emotional about the achievement of being awarded gold, 'It was hard work, long days, but worth every moment of it!' Perhaps most satisfying for the team was the wonderful feedback they received from members of the public. Sarah describes feeling 'quite inspired and uplifted' by the comments about the show garden, 'people seemed to really respond to the naturalness of it...many said they would love a garden like it themselves, or would like to change their gardens to create the same sort of effect.' Sarah was heartened that people were 'endorsing the desire for a natural environment', hoping that it might result in a wider ecological responsibility which 'always inspires' her.

So why was the Devon County Show such a resounding success for Docton Mill? Clearly because the garden on which the design was based has a unique atmosphere of its own, a naturalness that strikes a chord with visitors. This is a garden with a spell to weave, and like the enchanted Borretts, you won't want to leave in a hurry.

Enhancing Docton Mill's beauty and healthy ambiance is its stunning position. Located in a sheltered valley, just twenty minutes' walk from the spectacular coastal waterfall, Speke's Mouth, on North Devon's Hartland Peninsula, you would be hard-pressed to ask for a backdrop more conducive to the feeling of restfulness and seclusion which emanates from this garden. The Hartland Peninsula, itself designated an area of outstanding natural beauty, was all new for me, and I was really impressed by the sheer variety of its countryside. I admit I've always considered Devon just somewhere

vaguely pretty to travel through on the way to the real deal, my home, Cornwall. This was transparently a senseless bias because this region is well worth exploring; 17,000 acres of startling contrasts, from dramatic seascapes with towering cliff faces and views of Lundy Island, to ancient woodland and open moors.

The garden itself is designed to complement a restored mill of Saxon origin which featured in the Doomsday Book. Making much use of the mill's waterways, Docton is extensively planted and incredibly lush and green. A famous collection of magnolias is dedicated to Iris Pugh, who created the gardens in 1980; these look magnificent in spring and can be found in what is known as Caleb's Field. Caleb's Field is perhaps one of the more obviously designed areas within the naturalistic Docton Mill, its borders provide a paintbox of subtle tones of silver, purple, pink and blue. Planting, of course, is not just about colour—texture is also used to great effect.

The oddly rubbery foliage of succulents mixes with plants such as *Stachys byzantina* (aptly known as Lamb's Ear), which have gorgeous, velvety silver leaves that you just can't help but touch. Echiums along the back of the borders tower over everything else—looming alien presences with weird hairdos, some sort of punk beehive that only a plant could get away with. Vibrant lavender, some sort of variety that I'd never seen before (*Stoechas Lavender*), the flowers of which appear to have multiple black shiny eyes and bunny ears sprouting from their heads. It has to be said that visiting a garden as a horticultural ignoramus is a refreshing experience—it took a project like this to really remind me to look at my surroundings. And here at Docton Mill, I was amazed at both the beauty and the intrinsic strangeness of nature and all it can produce. Docton Mill's woodland walks set into the hillside give good views over the mill and the lower parts of the garden—plus the climb uses up some calories too (which can always be replaced at the tearooms).

In spring these pathways are awash with colour, a carpet of bluebells with a wallpaper of azaleas and rhododendrons, and armchairs of...hmm, this is getting needlessly metaphorical.

Perhaps my favourite visit to Docton was in April, when the garden had been invaded and completely conquered by daffodils—they were everywhere! The weather was perfect, the sky a bright blue in beautiful contrast to the sunny cheer of the yellow daffodils. Above the legions of flowers, the trees, still bare, held out skeletal fingers against the sky—a striking juxtaposition of the seemingly lifeless with the vitality of the daffodils in full bloom.

they were rather aggressive to visitors!' (Misanthropes may well think, 'fair enough', but everyone else reading should have no fear—the geese have left the garden.)

On occasion the wildlife has shared the garden with some more dubious characters. Alan Mort tells the story of an elderly visitor who was seemingly sweetness itself… Dissembling as physically impaired, the archetypical little old lady hobbled into the garden, where she quickly threw aside her walking stick, removed a trowel from her handbag and started digging up some choice plants. Warned by a witness to the crime, Alan accosted the thief. She denied all knowledge, but her bag full of expensive contraband was a dead giveaway.

So Fast Rabbit may have a few less rare and valuable plants on display—due to the antics of the larcenous ladies—but it is still an extraordinary garden with its own special atmosphere. A real favourite with the film crew, this is a private idyll, a place to relax and feel truly connected with the natural environment. Don't come to Fast Rabbit expecting a sterile space of precision vistas and planting; instead this is a garden bursting with life and vitality—one that fits in so well with its South Devon surroundings that it feels like it really belongs, and it's difficult to imagine the hard work behind its construction.

Only twenty minutes walk from beautiful coastline, with the popular Blackpool Sands and historic town of Dartmouth nearby, Fast Rabbit garden is a secret just waiting to be discovered.

The Really Wild Show

Wildlife to lookout for at Fast Rabbit Gardens:

Blackcaps

These like to nest in the garden's camellias. Slightly smaller than the House Sparrow, this warbler with a striking black or reddish-brown cap has a melodic fluting song that has earned it the name of 'northern Nightingale'.

Greenfinches

Resplendent in green and yellow, this very colourful character is frequently spotted flying in and out of the conifers in the rockery area of the garden. They have a wheezing song (probably asthmatic) and tend to squabble with other birds when feeding.

Song thrushes

Numbers of this popular songbird are in serious decline; the RSPB categorises it as a Red List species, meaning the conservation of its population is of the highest priority. Brown with a spotted belly, the song of this thrush is unusual in that it is often repetitive (just like my mother, it doesn't know when to change its tune).

Goldcrests

Moss green, with a creamy white underbelly and a distinctive yellow crest (a sort of punky centre parting), these are the smallest songbirds in the UK. Like the greenfinches, they can be found loitering around the garden's rockery. In April, if you're lucky, you might spot their nests in the conifers; these intricate, complex hammock-like structures take up to two weeks to build (but no planning permission required).

Kingfishers

The garden has a pair of resident kingfishers. These speed merchants are unmistakable with their brightly coloured blue and orange plumage. They love shallow still or slow-moving water, so Fast Rabbit's lake is an ideal location for them to find fish and aquatic insects to snack on.

Badgers

When I think of badgers, I think of the gruff, moody old character in 'The Wind in the Willows', but these animals can actually be wonderfully playful—cubs in particular are gregarious and, if you're very fortunate, dusk is the time to catch a glimpse of their mischief-making.

Foxes

When not being chased across the countryside by dogs and people on horses, foxes hang out at the garden in large numbers. No doubt the rabbit population is an attraction—fast food ('McRabbit'?) for the busy fox on the go.

© Rob Chace, 2007

Mink

The dreaded mink! A member of the weasel family and a relative of stoats, otters, polecats and badgers, the mink is not native but was introduced from North America to be bred commercially for its fur. Escapees have no natural predators, so they are thriving. Based on what I've heard from the guys at Fast Rabbit, they are the thugs of the animal world.

Hares

The brown hare is inexorably linked with the garden. Just like rabbits, hares are not rodents but lagomorphs. They differ from their cousins in terms of size—having a larger and longer body, much longer hind legs and longer black-tipped ears. In contrast to rabbits, the young of the hare (leverets) are born furred and with open eyes—this is lucky, as hares don't bother with burrows, merely residing in a shallow nest of grass known as a 'form'.

Rabbits

I'd be very surprised if you didn't see one of these at the garden. They are such a familiar sight, it's strange to think that they are not native to the UK.

Otters

Well, otter to be precise. Evidence of a solo otter has been found at the garden, but no one has yet been lucky enough to catch a glimpse of it. Obviously an elusive creature!

And that's not all, you could also see wrens, chaffinches, woodpeckers, blue tits, butterflies, dragonflies, damselflies, toads, newts, eels, voles, yetis, unicorns and sea monsters (okay, so I made the last three up...but you never know).

© Rob Chace, 2007

Go Wild

Want to encourage a few more critters into your own garden? Some advice from the Fast Rabbit team:

Choose tempting plants

Don't only choose plants that appeal to your own eye. Birds, bees and butterflies have their own favourites. At Fast Rabbit they have noticed that even the colour of the flower appears to be influential, 'yellow and orange seems to attract lots of insects.' In fact research suggests that bees have a preference for blue flowers. The garden has many gorgeous varieties of cultivated plants, such as the double-flowered Great White Cherry (or Tihaku), but, Alan warns, double flowers are not particularly wildlife friendly. Bees prefer single-flowered plants as they're much easier to collect nectar from.

Go native

Our native wildflowers and trees provide ideal habitats plus food for insects, which will in turn supply sustenance for larger forms of wildlife.

And finally...be messy!

Resist the urge to have the perfect, tidy garden. For instance, Fast Rabbit has a varying approach to grass cutting, and whilst main walkways are cut weekly, grassy slopes are left until late summer or early autumn time. Long grass provides habitats for insects, which are crucial if you want birds. The Fast Rabbit team reminds us that, 'encouraging wildlife isn't just about putting nest boxes up, it's about providing food for the young as well.' When the grass is cut from the slopes it is turned and allowed to dry over a few days, Alan explains, 'this allows seed of wildflowers to fall out of the grass to germinate at a later

date and the cut grass is then collected as hay and fed to sheep or composted.' Also try to avoid the temptation to clear the garden completely of deadwood and fallen leaves. These areas are beloved of insect life, plus any rotting that occurs will help to fertilise the soil.

A piece of folklore for you: apparently it's a good idea to stamp on the first daisy of the season to protect loved ones. If you don't, they are likely to be pushing up the daisies themselves by the year's end. (But please make sure you only destroy the plant life in your own garden!)

Highlights

Spring is in the Air...

This is the season not to miss at Fast Rabbit. Bluebells carpet the woodland trails, and a plethora of lesser known wildflowers—celandine, speedwell, primrose and wood violet to name just a few—flourish here. Spring is also the time to see Fast Rabbit's more exotic element—from rhododendrons and camellias to delicate cherry blossoms. Plus the Bog Garden also looks its best, with the unusual, slightly freaky-looking skunk cabbage out in force. The large leaves of this plant give off a strong smell of rotten meat when bruised or crushed, which attracts insects—so don't get too close!

Did I mention the wildlife?

Fast Rabbit Farm Garden, Ash Cross, Nr Dartmouth, Devon, TQ6 0LR, 01803 712437

www.fastrabbitfarm.co.uk

BICTON PARK BOTANICAL GARDENS

Budleigh Salterton, Devon

Exotic   Italianate   Magnificent   Family adventure

Walking into Bicton is like walking back in time; the garden is so perfectly representative of another era, it resonates with voices and tales from the past. When wandering across the lawns of the Italian Garden, it is easy to imagine encountering characters from the garden's beginnings in the 18th century.

Perhaps one of the most influential figures involved with Bicton was Lady Louisa Rolle. Interestingly, Louisa was not one to kowtow to the epoch's expectations of female gender—the evidence suggests that the words 'meek' and 'mild' were not part of her vocabulary, let alone her nature. Strong, determined, exacting, she was described as a 'woman without equal' and as a 'female rival of Alexander the Great'; indeed, it was suggested that she went further than the aforementioned conqueror, subjugating both hemispheres in her gardens. This resulted in an incredibly ambitious collection of trees and shrubs from far-flung places, the like of which had rarely been seen on UK soil.

The 28-year-old Louisa got her hands on Bicton estate via marriage in 1822 to Lord John Rolle, a man 38 years her senior (so she was probably glad to have the gardens to expend her energies on). Apparently this huge generation gap was bridged by the couple's shared love for Bicton's gardens; adding to the Italian Garden, which had been laid out in 1735 by the first Baron Rolle, they shaped the way the garden looks today. To show his love for Louisa, John gave her the Palm House—considered one of the world's most beautiful garden buildings, and so much better than a gift voucher! She may have expected diamonds, but John was certainly no cheapskate—window tax was not to be abolished until 1845 and glass was extremely expensive. The Palm House dates from around 1825-30 and therefore predates the one at the Royal Botanic Gardens at Kew. Despite its curvy splendour, it is actually glazed with flat glass, enabled by using 18,000 very small panes. Louisa was also generous with her gifts to her husband, giving him a whole church, St Mary's, built in 1850—but only after his death in 1842. Let's hope he appreciated it!

She lived on, as the richest woman in Devon, until her death in 1885 a few days before her 90th birthday, presumably only pausing in her horticulturalist pursuits to do a spot of libelling. The subject of her libellous attacks is another important figure in Bicton's history—head gardener James Barnes. Apparently Victorian head gardeners had formidable reputations as strict disciplinarians, and Barnes (1806-1877) was no exception. Describing Bicton as a 'shambles' when he first started work at the gardens in 1840, he quickly introduced a barrage of rules to keep his employees in order. The rule board can be seen on the wall near the Mediterranean Garden and includes such gems as: 'Any man found at his work intoxicated shall forfeit his day's wages and be otherwise dealt with as thereafter shall be considered just', as well as strong indictments against 'evil expressions' and 'going into any hothouse, greenhouse...or walking on any gravel path with dirty shoes' (a bit harsh surely in this line of work). Barnes established a system of fines for those who dared break the rules, causing much resentment as he notes in his journal, 'It was said that my long ugly legs would not be walking Bicton gardens long.' No wonder the under-gardeners were peeved, as Barnes wrote, 'They were never satisfied unless they were guzzling or smoking', and fines of up to one shilling out of a weekly wage of 10-15 shillings (equivalent to £20-30 today) must have made a dent in their alcohol funds. Happily, however, at the end of the year the amount raised by the fines was shared equally between the workers—meaning they were free to drink themselves silly.

Despite initial glum mutterings, Barnes earned the respect of his gardeners and the effect on Bicton in his words was 'truly astonishing', his endeavours earning the gardens admiration across the UK. In his thirty years of employment at Bicton, diligent Barnes rejuvenated the garden—updating tools and conceiving new ways to improve compost (adding charcoal to prevent it from becoming too acidic)—yet it seems it wasn't enough for his boss. Louisa Rolle was alleged to be an autocrat and was known to have offended some of her employees with her high-handed manner. In 1869, following Barnes's retirement, she wrote him a letter

about the offending tree, Bicton staff declared it obvious, 'it's the ugly one in the Pinetum', and suspiciously offered no other assistance. I couldn't help thinking it was all a myth—what's an ugly tree anyway? Who decides whether trees are good-looking or not? I've heard of tree huggers, but tree insulters? So actually I lied about the Ugly Tree being 'best of all'—Bicton has plenty more to offer.

Inspired by the French designer Andre Le Notre, creator of the gardens at Versailles, the formal Italian Garden is particularly special; exceptional not just because of its precise

accusing him of leaving Bicton in a 'disorderly' state. Barnes was so enraged by this that he took her to court for libel, winning the pretty decent sum of £200 (which would work out to about £8,500 today). This somewhat unexpected outcome elevated levels of respect for professional gardeners throughout the country—no doubt it was also heartening news for anyone who didn't happen to reside in a gigantic country house.

Bicton Botanical Gardens are remarkable for being a perfectly conserved time capsule, with a fine Italian Garden, the aforementioned Palm House, and a multitude of unusual or record-holding flora and trees. And best of all, as marked on the map, Bicton has the Ugly Tree. The Ugly Tree quickly became my nemesis at the garden; numerous attempts to locate it failed, our photographers and camera operators all searched in vain. When questioned

proportions and carefully aligned focal points, or its contemporary use of floral colour, but because of its very existence. Originally, the garden was designed to complement Bicton House, a Tudor mansion built after the original medieval manor was demolished in 1560. When the Tudor-style house was torn down in 1750 the garden was left untouched. By the end of the 18th century, however, fashions had changed radically—formal gardens were out, naturalistic landscaped 'Capability Brown' gardens were in. Fortunately, the current Bicton House was built away from the Italian Garden, with its own landscaped areas added to reflect the tastes of the times. Thus the Italian Garden survived as a monument to gardening history—simply because it was hidden from Bicton House and so couldn't offend style gurus of the period.

"...enough children's activities to exhaust even the most hyperactive youngster."
'The Independent'

"Impressive"
Peter Conchie's verdict on the 60 acres of gardens at Bicton ('The Independent')

Known as the Hermitage Garden, the landscaped area is a perfect place to relax—a retreat from the outside world. A lovely lake makes an ideal picnicking spot (on its banks mind, not in it). There's also a striking collection of dwarf conifers and heathers—brilliant if the big versions make you feel insecure about your height. And of course there's the newly restored Hermitage itself. A strange concept, this Victorian building dating from 1839 basically existed to give guests a good laugh. A common sight in grand gardens long before Louisa decided she wanted one to amuse herself with, early renditions were often built merely of tree roots, branches and roofed with moss. It is not known whether Louisa followed the practice of paying someone to live there, as a kind of professional hermit, but many landowners did so. I'm sure she wouldn't have been able to resist a giggle at some unkempt loner, and I suppose a home in beautiful Bicton takes the bite out of being sniggered at by posh people for a living.

Despite the acclaim for Louisa Rolle's...er...role in the creation of Bicton's famous horticultural collection, she didn't actually involve herself in any risky expeditions. Wealthy enthusiasts like Louisa made plant hunting a lucrative industry for nurseries such as Veitch's in nearby Exeter. Plant hunters—well known examples being Cornishman William Lobb and Ernest 'Chinese' Wilson—were the Indiana Joneses of their era, suffering untold hardships (and probably told ones too) all for the sake of an unusual or exotic species of plant or tree. Incongruous really to imagine what these guys went through to bring back, for example, a lily—not a very macho trophy is it? Looking at the pictures, they don't seem to bear any resemblance to Harrison Ford either. Nevertheless, Wilson was nothing if not intrepid, narrowly escaping death in the mountains of China whilst searching for the Regal Lily, breaking his leg in two places to be left with what he referred to as his

'lily limp'. A very successful plant hunter with over 1,000 introductions to his credit, he has a collection in the Lower Pinetum at Bicton named in his honour. The Handkerchief Tree (*Davidia involucrate*), one of Bicton's most visually unusual trees, and so named for its fluttery white flowers, was one that he brought back from China after several misadventures. Nearly imprisoned as a spy during the Boxer Rebellion, avoiding the Bubonic Plague in Hong Kong, and surviving a terrifying journey through the storm-swollen rapids of the Yangtze River in which many men drowned, Ernest certainly had an interesting life. Not one to complain about his sufferings either, he wrote: 'Such count for nothing, since I have lived in nature's boundless halls and drank deeply of her pleasures. To wander through a tropical or temperate forest with tree trunks more stately than a gothic column, beneath a canopy of foliage more lovely in its varied forms than the roof of any building fashioned by man...where does hardship figure when the reward is such?'

Looking around Bicton, it is noticeable that a wide variety of people of all ages enjoy the garden. Horticultural enthusiasts have a diverse range of botanicals to look at: a collection of over 1,000 trees in the landscaped area; the American Garden (established in the 1830s for New World species and containing some of Bicton's loveliest trees); the Mediterranean Garden; and several glasshouses, including the constantly humid and warm Tropical House—ideal conditions for orchids and bananas to flourish. The Arid House is home to an array of weird and wonderful cacti, and the Temperate House has colour all year round, however bleak the weather, with stunning favourites such as geraniums, fuchsias and begonias.

But it's not just the plant spotters that come to Bicton; the Italian lawns offer a relaxing venue for a little sunbathing or exercise to anyone of any age, and the gardens have made a special effort to provide facilities to entertain the young. A scenic ride by train is available—fun for kids (although one boy complained to me that it was too slow, I think he was missing the point of a 'scenic' journey somewhat) and fantastic for the perpetually exhausted or lazy. For children there're also playgrounds, mini-golf, an indoor play area for rainy days and somewhere to feed them (in the impressive Temple Orangey) when they need reviving.

Education and conservation are key goals for the garden. The Bicton Orchid Conservation Project serves both purposes by enlisting science students from a secondary comprehensive school to assist in safeguarding endangered species. The students propagate sustainable cultivated seedlings in their school laboratory to raise funds to help conserve orchids in Central America and to reduce the unsustainable demand for plants taken from the wild. These seedlings can be purchased at the gift shop and you can even buy your very own Bicton orchid (*Lemboglossum bictoniense*). Part of botanical history, this previously unknown orchid was cultivated at Bicton in 1836 and examples of it can be found in the Tropical House. Easy to grow, it flowers in autumn with long-lasting pink or white 'lips' and is just as admirably alien looking (in my opinion) as other orchids.

Plant names, clockwise starting from top left: Ornamental pepper, *Capsicum annuum* 'Masquerade'; Lobster Claws bromeliad, *vriesea carinata*; Orchid; Agave, *Agave potatorum*; Bromeliad, *Aechmea fasciata*; Frangipani, *Plumeria alba*; Bromeliad, *Guzmania lingulata* 'Minor'; Bromeliad, *Neoregelia carolinae* 'Tricolor'; Prickly Pear, *Opuntia bergeriana*.

Bicton: the Garden for Every Season

Unlike many gardens, Bicton is open throughout the year (but probably not on Christmas Day, so you'll have to celebrate it surrounded by psychotic family members again—or is that just me?). The gardens are open across the seasons; they have something special to offer whatever the weather or time of year.

Spring

Rhododendrons, camellias and blossoms all provide vivid colour in spring. May is the time to see the unusual Handkerchief Tree in flower, as well as the *Wisteria*—which at approximately 180 years is reportedly the oldest in the country.

Summer

One of my favourites, the Tulip Tree, shows off...yes you guessed it...tulip-like flowers in midsummer. Bicton has a fantastic example of this type of tree—extremely tall, it gave our photographers a hard time trying to capture images of its pale, delicate flowers. The herbaceous borders in the Italian Garden look especially glorious in summer, and late in the season is the time to catch the Mediterranean Garden.

Autumn

An array of trees really perform in the autumn—including the Tupelo and Sweetgum, both hailing from North America, plus the ever popular maples. This is also the time to see Bicton's own orchid in flower.

Winter

The formal structure of the Italian Garden, with its lake and fountains, is starkly beautiful in winter, and if you're desperate for flora there's always something to see in Bicton's glasshouses. If the weather's out to get you, then there're plenty of places to hide, from the Shell House, with its comprehensive collection of shells, to the Countryside Museum with its agricultural exhibits...or you could always pop into the church and pray for less inclement weather.

Highlights

The Ugly Tree

A highlight, only if you can find it.

The Cacti

I was unaware that there was so much variety amongst cacti—the Arid House at Bicton is the perfect showcase for it. Fearsome spikes and delicate flowers, this is surely a good starting point for curious children if you want to show them something horticultural (if you can get them away from the play areas).

Bigger, Better, Older

Due to Louisa Rolle's ambitious horticultural desires, Bicton has a world-famous collection of trees and shrubs. In the internationally acclaimed Pinetum, there are 25 'champions' that hold records for their size; a delight for everyone who truly believes size matters. Some wellingtonias and coast redwoods at Bicton have reached heights of over 35 metres!

Bicton Park Botanical Gardens, East Budleigh, Budleigh Salterton, Devon, EX9 7BJ, 01395 568465
www.bictongardens.co.uk

COTHAY MANOR GARDENS

Nr Wellington, Somerset

Romantic   Medieval   Subtle   Fairytale   Mystifying

Cothay Manor is a stunning sight, considered by many to be the most perfect of small, classic, medieval buildings in England today. In fact, it rates four stars in Simon Jenkins' 'England's Thousand Best Houses'. Built in 1485, virtually untouched and in remarkably good condition, it is amazing to think that places like this exist and still stranger that they are considered home to those who dwell in them. It seems bizarre in today's society to imagine unloading your supermarket shopping in a residence that must surely have a princess or two imprisoned in a tower somewhere.

Cothay Manor, and its surrounding 12 acres of gardens, is indeed straight out of a fairytale. And, in the illusionary manner of fairytales, it is a real devil to find. The literature concerning Cothay describes the manor as remaining 'hidden for centuries' and that's certainly no surprise. Wryly, the directions on the garden's website note that the mile from the main road to Cothay will 'feel like ten'. However, sometimes there is more to be gained from something that requires an effort to be made. Cothay is the perfect example of this; its relative obscurity adds to its charm, making visitors feel all the more privileged to immerse themselves in its magic.

The gardens at Cothay were laid out in the 1920s by Colonel Reginald Cooper (the oldest friend of Harold Nicholson, who created the garden at Sissinghurst with his wife Vita Sackville-West). It is easy to assume that the inspiration for Cothay—now often described as 'the Sissinghurst of the West' arose from the more famous garden. However, as Alastair Robb notes, 'it was actually the other way round' as Sissinghurst was laid out later, work beginning in the 1930s.

However, the association between the two gardens is obvious; Cothay is similarly made up of many garden 'rooms', each leading off from a central structure of a 200-yard yew walk.

Over the past 10 years, the gardens, within the original

structures of the yew hedges, have been completely re-designed and planted by Alastair and his wife Mary-Anne. The couple have a wealth of knowledge to draw upon as they are both from horticultural backgrounds. Alastair's great-grandmother (another Mary-Anne) was a plant hunter—the spurge *Euphorbia amygdaloides* 'var. robbiae' is named after her (nicknamed Mrs Robb's Bonnet because she had to hide it in her hat to smuggle it through customs!). The present Mary-Anne Robb has always had a passion for flowers, and her mother was a keen, very knowledgeable gardener.

Alastair Robb concentrates on the structure and proportions whilst Mary-Anne is a skilled plantswoman and is responsible for the dreamy, ethereal ambience of the garden. Alastair explains, 'Lots of gardeners go for a melange of colour, but she goes for a graduation of tone, very subtle colours, nothing over-bright.' His pride in his wife's talents is rather endearing—he is keen for her to write a book on her speciality, planting up large pots (other literature on this subject he describes as 'deadly boring'), in which she sometimes uses up to an impressive 48 plants per pot.

When the Robb family first acquired Cothay, the gardens were, in Alastair Robb's words, 'well manicured but not gardened'. He clarifies that although the yew hedges were smartly clipped, they had elder, box, sycamore and brambles growing in them. They must have been growing in the hedges for years because when they were cut out, and the roots removed, gaping holes were left, some of which are still repairing today. With so many challenges to overcome, it is transparently clear how much work has gone into making Cothay Manor Gardens look the way they do today. It has all been too much for some employees: two burly Australian students helped swap the concrete flagstones on the terrace for stone ones, and were then desperate to vanish back to Australia! However, current gardener Wesley is not so easily daunted; when asked if he minds

slogging away day after day to maintain the gardens, he replied, 'It's a holiday'. There is a real tranquillity here in this hidden corner of Somerset, and it is no wonder that there's nowhere he'd rather be.

If you had to choose one word to describe Cothay it would be 'romantic'. This, in part, can be ascribed to the ancient ambiance that still pervades the house and gardens. The rose, a flower which in England has more romantic connotations than any other, has played a colourful role in Cothay's history. The rent for the land surrounding the manor in the medieval era was a pair of silver spurs and a rose—a pleasingly eccentric payment. Legend tells us that to celebrate the end of the War of the Roses, a red rose and a white rose were planted on the terrace by Richard Bluett, who was the lord of the manor at the time. The Robbs keep the memory of this legend alive—you can still see the red rose of Lancaster and the white rose of York flowering at Cothay today.

It all started, of course, in the clay pit—which is now the Woodland Garden. This features an array of plants that enjoy shade and dappled light, and is best enjoyed in the spring when the whole area is carpeted by wildflowers such as bluebells, wood violets and celandines, whilst huge rhododendrons bestow more dramatic colour. Nearby is the Bog Garden, which looks so true to its name that it is easy to imagine a hippo or two emerging from its muddy waters. The pond is surrounded by a veritable jungle of moisture-loving plants, from ferns and candelabra primulas to the very recognisable—with its strong oval-shaped foliage and bright yellow flowers—stinky old favourite, the skunk cabbage.

The Pergola Walk, with its straight lines and statue as a focal point, was the first area designed by Mary in a formal style; yet it retains the pleasing informality that characterises the garden as a whole. Roses and geraniums have been pretty much allowed to do their own thing—and they do so abundantly. Indeed, Mary's favourite gardening tip concerns how to achieve a relaxed planting scheme, 'I think if you're trying to create a very natural feel in your garden it is important to have self seeders, because however you place the things, nature is able to put them in such good places itself, and if you have these self seeders round the garden you get an intermingling of plants which I personally like very much.' For fans of the cottage garden style, both the Courtyard and Terrace Gardens will please. Brim full of flowering perennials that bloom in June and July, they help provide a vibrantly colourful spectacle throughout the summer.

Burrow Farm is certainly a garden of contrasts, but despite its fusion of styles it doesn't ever appear at odds with the beauty of its Devonshire surroundings, the design never seems forced or contrived. It is Mary's affinity with her natural environment, her true love of her vocation and her quiet enthusiasm that imbue the gardens with their considerable charm—and you can't help hoping that she doesn't stop here, and maybe pinches just one more small piece of farmland when the cows have their backs turned!

Mary's experience is also invaluable in her popular plant nursery, where she is often on hand to offer advice. Many of the plants on show in her garden can be found for sale, so the visitor can take home a little piece of Burrow Farm without resorting to nefarious tactics (see Fast Rabbit).

Certain plants, however, have more uses than simply sitting pretty in your back garden. It's always a shame to hear that NASA aren't making any progress discovering monsters from other worlds, but nevertheless it was their early research that revealed the remarkable pollution-tackling qualities of plants. It was discovered that in airtight space habitats, common houseplants are very effective at absorbing toxic VOCs (volatile organic chemicals). Later studies have found that the indoor environment is likely to be five to seven times more polluted than the atmosphere outside, often due to VOCs emitted from modern furnishings and technology, such as photocopiers and printers. Formaldehyde, for instance, is released from adhesives, carpets and tobacco smoke and can affect asthma and cause respiratory difficulties.

Lucky, then, that the horticultural world contains some superheroes. And it appears to be spider plant rather than Spiderman to the rescue; placed in a small enclosed space it has the ability to remove 96% of poisonous carbon monoxide from the air. Varieties of *Dracaena*, the Peace lily, the Boston fern, the rubber plant and the attractive flowering *Gerbera*, are all species that can be kept indoors and will increase your sense of wellbeing—so why not buy a few pot plants instead of biscuits to take to the office?

As well as physical benefits, such as the absorption of noise and the cleansing and purification of air, houseplants have also been proven to be beneficial psychologically. Simply by their presence, plants have the ability to increase positive feelings and reduce feelings of anxiety, anger and sadness. And if you find your attention wondering during the day, they can also improve concentration and memory skills, whilst alleviating stress and encouraging feelings of calm and tranquillity. If a few spider plants in your sitting room can do all that, think how good you'll feel after a visit to Burrow Farm!

"Given a choice, people sit where they can see plants."
(One of the findings of an Oxford Brooks University study by Jane Stiles in 1995. However, given the choice, seven out of ten people refuse to relocate to the midst of the jungle-filled Congo Basin. I don't know…people are fickle.)

Sometimes known as the Tibetan cherry or Mahogany bark cherry, this is one of several truly beautiful trees in the garden. This cherry's most striking feature is its glossy, rich red-brown bark. Looking like someone has encircled a red ribbon around its trunk, the metallic sheen makes you just want to reach out and touch it. In fact, Mary has positioned it close to the garden's entrance so many visitors do so—possibly giving it a polish in the process. In early spring, delicate white flowers are produced which beautifully offset the vivid bark.

Highlights

A Very Personal Journey

'A garden that one makes oneself becomes associated with one's personal history...interwoven with one's tastes, preferences and character, and constitutes a sort of unwritten autobiography. Show me your garden, provide it be your own, and I will tell you what you are like.'
Alfred Austin (1835-1913)

Damn it, someone always manages to say precisely what I want to say before me—and in much posher prose too!

The Family Business

Mary's grandson reeling off never-ending Latin plant names, such as *Metasequoia glptostroboides* or *Acer palmatum* 'Dissectum Nigrum', seems somehow shocking from the mouth of a eight-year-old—especially to this horticulturally ignorant writer. She's taught him well; now I wonder if she can teach me a way to remember the spelling of rhododendron? (I have a battle with my spell check facility every time.)

Prunus serrula

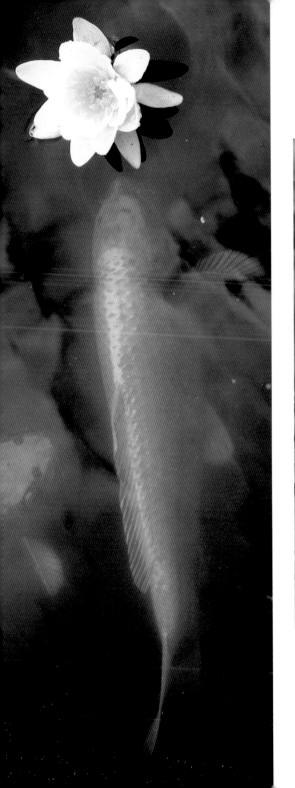

Burrow Farm Gardens, Dalwood, Axminster, Devon, EX13 7ET, 01404 831285
www.burrowfarmgardens.co.uk

MORETON GARDENS

Moreton, Dorset

Elusive   Multifaceted   Famous connections   Rural

In a curiously understated grave behind the tranquil Moreton Gardens lies the enigmatic T. E. Lawrence, otherwise known as Lawrence of Arabia. The pleasant village of Moreton, deep in Hardy's green and pastoral Dorset, seems as far removed from the vast, barren desert landscapes that Lawrence loved so passionately as could be possible. So how did he come to be buried here?

Richard Frampton Hobbs, describing Lawrence as 'vaguely a cousin', explains: 'Lawrence of Arabia as many will know, having come back form the desert as a hero, was not a hero sort of guy. He didn't like being a hero; he spent much of the rest of his life trying to get away from the press, a familiar story for many these days…And he succeeded quite well. He rented a cottage from us, Clouds Hill, and unfortunately for him whilst driving too fast, as was his habit, on his motorbike he swerved to avoid two boys on cycles and died a few days later as a result of his injuries. His mother rang my family and asked if he could be buried here—and it's as simple as that. That's why Lawrence of Arabia, national hero, is buried in the small village of Moreton.'

Despite a plethora of biographies, Lawrence remains an elusive character. Ambitious, supremely intelligent, he emerged from WW1 as a celebrated figure—admired for his role in uniting the Arabs and assisting them in the 1916-1918 revolt against the Turkish. He took an unconventional route to success; eschewing the camaraderie of the officers' mess, he achieved the rank of Lieutenant Colonel whilst

remaining without any regimental affiliation, on the Special List. Then, at the height of his fame, he simply walked away. Seemingly preferring obscurity, he enlisted as a private, the lowliest rank available, in the Army's Tank Corps. As he said in a letter to his friend D. G. Hogarth, 'I've finished with the "Lawrence" episode. I don't like what rumour makes of him—not the sort of man I'd like to be.'

Lawrence of Arabia isn't the only illustrious character in Frampton's ancestry. There's also James Frampton, who was notable for 'doing a Scarlet Pimpernel' and rescuing members of the aristocracy during the French Revolution of the late 18th century. When he returned to England, he was disturbed to find that workers were forming societies and feared a rebellion similar to the one he had experienced whilst in France.

In 1834, as Sheriff of Dorset, he arrested the group who would later become renowned as the Tolpuddle Martyrs. The six men were convicted and sent to Australia for signing a secret oath as members of the Friendly Society of Agricultural Labourers, which was a sort of early trade union. Richard is aware public opinion would be likely to side with the martyrs these days, as he points out with a smile, 'certainly the family name is associated on the wrong side of that particular issue.'

An ancestor Richard is a little less ambivalent about is

a man by the name of Tregunnel Frampton. Not only was he the founder of Newmarket Racecourse but he held the position of Keeper of the King's Horses during the reign of four monarchs—assisted, as Richard makes clear, by 'three of those monarchs dieing pretty quickly', it is nevertheless an unrivalled record.

> **"All men dream: but not equally. Those who dream by night in the dusty recesses of their minds wake in the day to find that it was vanity; but the dreamers of the day are dangerous men, for they may act out their dream with open eyes, to make it possible."**
> T. E. Lawrence. from 'Seven Pillars of Wisdom'

And if that all isn't impressive enough, Richard also has a signed confession from one of the murderers of the notorious Rasputin (Russia's greatest love machine) in his family vault. As Richard divulges, 'One of my ancestors at the time was the Ambassador to Norway and one of the princes made his escape from Russia and presented himself at the British Embassy in Oslo for protection. He then sat down and gave a written statement of precisely what happened—so while there are a lot of rumours and an awful lot is indeed known in detail about what happened, we have fairly safely secured in our possession a very detailed account and we intend to

release it on the 100th anniversary of Rasputin's death so that everybody can have the benefit of it.'

So what's any of this got to do with gardens? I don't know really, I just found it interesting. But when you consider just how intertwined the history of Moreton is with Richard's ancestry, you do get a sense of why it is such a special location. He isn't entirely sure of exactly how long his family have resided in the area, 'but it's pretty much as long as anyone in Dorset. We certainly go back to the 13th century—the earliest known Frampton, who was a Norman, was given Moreton by the king.' And because Moreton has been part of the Frampton estate solidly since the 1300s, very little has changed; it has not needed to modernise and has remained the embodiment of the picture-perfect Dorset village. This might mean the locals yearn for amenities (they all look like they're crying out for a UCI multiplex to me), but it makes the place all the more endearing to visitors.

Lawrence's grave is perhaps Moreton's chief attraction with its solemn inscription: 'The hour is coming and now is when the dead shall hear the voice of the son of God and they that hear shall live.' It cites Lawrence as a fellow of All Souls College, Oxford, like that was his major achievement, giving no hint of his triumphs that brought him celebrity. Surreally, a dish can be found right behind his tombstone, filled with little fish-shaped cat food. It all seems strangely unassuming, a resting place unpretentious in the extreme for such a hero. But perhaps he would have preferred it that way.

Lawrence's funeral service was conducted in the village church, St Nicolas' and was attended by many of the most important and influential people of the time, and Winston Churchill. The church is definitely worth a visit with its unusual engraved windows. And if you're hungry for more Lawrence, then stop for refreshment at the tearooms. Filled with Lawrence memorabilia, including what is darkly referred to as his last set of wheels, his coffin trolley, the

tearooms are housed in a charmingly rustic building which once served as the village school.

So with all that there is to see in Moreton, why bother visiting the gardens? Lawrence once expressed the wish to be known for his writing rather than his WWI exploits, and like any artist, he drew on his surroundings for inspiration. Tom Penny, a landscape gardener, currently leases the E-shaped wall garden of about 6.5 acres; it has the gardens on one side, and on the other, the nurseries where Tom and his family grow most of their own plants—which are available from the nearby Plant Centre. Tom feels that the gardens have a special 'aura', an appeal that he was struck by instantly when he first viewed them several years ago. 'Gardens are meant to be relaxing, but Moreton is more than that…it's inspiring.'

The garden is a Mecca for artists; they are especially keen to capture the natural beauty of the river walk with its Monet-style bridge. Gently winding paths travel through woodland, a profuse jungle of hostas, ferns and hydrangeas, past a bog garden boasting an abundance of water lovers such as vividly coloured candelabra *Primula*, *Gunnera* and daylilies, and out to the sunnier and lighter surroundings of the formal garden with its *Wisteria* covered pergola, and long vistas.

This is a garden full of contrasts: The symmetry of the formal areas, with a fountain and a sundial as focal points adding structure to the garden; whilst the wilder areas are a haven for wildlife and have a soothing, softening effect on the garden as a whole. Visitors can enjoy some shade in the Jubilee Summer House on the lawn; rather nicely, it has been constructed using reclaimed materials—oak from trees that have fallen on the estate and a floor built from Commonwealth war grave headstones.

A newer area is the Font Garden. Merely a large patch of earth when this project began a year or so ago, it is now overflowing with colour and texture. It features abundant planting around a font which mirrors the design of the one in the nearby church and is likewise made of Portland stone.

For Tom, Moreton Gardens illustrates how water plays a crucial role in garden design. 'Moreton gardens are built around water, a natural stream that flows through. Water is key to most gardens; it encourages extra wildlife, and allows a variety of water-loving plants which contrast beautifully with the traditional type of plant.' Wildlife is actively encouraged at Moreton, the wide variety of planting is obviously appealing to butterflies—many different types, some relatively rare, enrich the gardens with their colourful presence. Tom adds some other inhabitants to the list, 'we have stoats, we have ducks and moorhens, we have mistle thrushes which are quite scarce these days, linnets and goldfinches…It goes to show that a garden is a natural habitat for wildlife in any area—it can be city or country.'

From the diversity in garden styles, from formalistic to naturalistic, and the wealth of vibrantly coloured flowers and textured foliage, it's easy to forget that this is a garden, at least in horticultural terms, in its infancy. Yet Moreton Gardens is not without a long history. The gardens are at the heart of the Moreton estate and were originally laid out in 1742. Both the stone walls that encircle the garden and an octagonal building, the bothy, where young boys employed as gardeners probably lived, are original features. Owner Richard is positive that the gardens go back even further, 'we'd love to know what happened in the 15th and 16th centuries and there was certainly something here because the original large estate house was Elizabethan and there would have been something else before that.' Unfortunately no records exist and this part of the garden's past remains a mystery. During the Victorian era the garden was both ornamental and productive, filled with greenhouses and fruit trees and busy providing food for the 'big house'. The 'Dig for Victory' campaign of the Second World War meant that food production was imperative and it wasn't practical for the garden to retain a decorative element.

However, in 1997 it was decided that the garden should be restored to something similar to its original format (as far as its owners can tell!) for the public to enjoy. Tom has great plans for the garden, hoping to 'improve on what is already marvellous' by creating new areas. First on his list is a 'corner of shapes and sculptures using natural shapes of trees, stumps and objects like that incorporated into textured planting—because after all, plants are more foliage than they are flower, therefore one has to use that texture.' There is the sense that these gardens are at the heart of a united community that resolutely refuses to forget its history and its values. Both serene and soulful, a garden to create in, to be inspired by.

The Butterfly Effect

Butterflies have been the subject of more books than any other animal, excepting birds. Why do we love them so much? Obviously they have a seemingly fragile beauty that appeals to many, but what do we actually know about them? And what is the difference between a butterfly and a moth?

I remember being told as a child that butterflies have fairy dust on their wings—and that you must not touch them in case the dust comes off on your fingers rendering the creatures flightless. The delicate nature of the butterfly is often emphasised, after all they do seem the graceful ballerinas of the Animal Kingdom. However, they are in fact one of the most successful animal groups in the world. The reason for their success is probably closely connected, I think, with why they are so enchanting. They are fascinatingly diverse, which means that they are rarely in competition with each other. They come in a range of sizes, shapes, colours and patterns, with species differing from one another as eggs, caterpillars and chrysalides and adults. Even metamorphosis takes place at different times of the year depending on the species, and each feeds on different types of plant.

Apparently, there is very little scientific value to a division between butterflies and moths. Yes, moths tend to be less colourful, fly at night with their wings flat (whilst butterflies fold their wings upright over their backs) and have straight or feathery antennae (as opposed to clubbed antennae). However, there are a huge number of exceptions, including butterflies that fly during the night and brightly coloured moths such as the shockingly pink Elephant Hawkmoth. Butterflies and moths have many enemies, which is the reason for their patterns and colourations—the provision of camouflage.

Moths seem to excel in this in really quite a freaky way. The Puss Moth, for instance is well named (it's grey and tabby just like a cat), whilst the Hummingbird Hawkmoth really resembles a Mini-Me version of the real thing, and the Buff Tip looks unbelievably like a twig or a wood chip. A garden is an ideal place to indulge an interest in these amazingly varied insects—just don't go all creepy and start catching them in bottles and pinning them to boards. Look out for these varieties, all found in the UK.

The Common Blue

As its name suggests, this is the blue butterfly that you are most likely to see. The male is the most colourful (typical vanity) being light blue finely framed with black. What's interesting about this species is it is one of several which, when in the vulnerable caterpillar stage, enlist ants as bodyguards. They secrete a substance that the ants relish so much that they, in the words of David Attenborough, 'look after the caterpillar with the solicitude of a farmer caring for a cow.'

Small Copper

These are copper coloured (yes the clue is in the name) and are the psychos of the butterfly world. The males are so territorial that they will even chase birds away.

The Magpie

A brightly coloured moth common throughout the whole of Europe. Yellow with black spots and poisonous! So...just don't eat too many.

Orange Tip

Fairly common in gardens, this white butterfly with striking orange patches on the end of its wings has an alarming habit. Any butterfly reading might want to stop reading right now as the truth may disturb. This butterfly is out to get you—a cannibal with a taste for any eggs or caterpillars that it comes across whilst munching on its favoured plants.

Highlights

The Butterflies

An abundance of these to be found in the garden—a testament to the thought put into the planting. Grab a guide from the shop and see how many varieties you can spot.

See the Light

Visit the church; the engraved windows make such a difference to the atmosphere, filling the space with light and creating a real sense of peace and warmth. Rather luckily for the church, its original windows were destroyed when it came under fire in the Second World War. Renowned artist Laurence Whistler (yet another Laurence!) designed the unique replacements.

Fording the Ford

Reportedly the longest ford in the South of England at over 80 metres wide, it has a lovely old footbridge going across it for those who don't like getting their feet wet, and miles of forestry walks beyond. On hot summer days it becomes quite a festive place to be: children and dogs cool off in its waters, horses and riders wade through (at least the horses do, it isn't that deep), and ducks frolic about doing... whatever ducks do.

The Lawrence Connection

So many myths and rumours about this character and his achievements. Fascinating to look for clues in the place he chose to hide from the world. And talking of myths, the story about the rose placed on his grave every year by a mysteriously anonymous person...disappointingly untrue. So why not go put one there yourself?

Moreton Gardens, Moreton, Dorset, DT2 8RF, 01929 405084
www.moretondorset.co.uk

COMPTON ACRES

Poole, Dorset

Eclectic   Unconventional   Incongruous   Pleasing   Oasis

Compton Acres, a series of snack-sized gardens that won't ruin your appetite. According to Peter Thoday, top horticulturist, Compton Acres 'started life as one man's passion in the 1920s', and he describes creator W. Simpson as 'an amateur' and a 'restless soul'. After surrounding his house with what was then a typically English garden, Simpson had obviously caught gardening fever and went on to build 'a necklace of gardens around that core which have become the famous Compton Acres set of five unusual places.' These consist of the Japanese Garden, the Italian Garden, the Wooded Valley, the Rock Garden and the Cacti Garden (which became the Heather Garden after WW2). It is this somewhat incongruous collection of 'rooms outside' that makes Compton Acres so special and, as Peter notes, to describe the gardens as 'eclectic is to underplay their eccentricity.'

Today Compton Acres is a popular oasis set smack bang within the bustling town of Poole. Successive owners have made their mark on Compton. It now has twelve separately themed gardens, including the Palm Court with its tall, shady palms and cool, soothing atmosphere; the Winter Garden which houses beautifully textured contemporary African sculptures; and the Garden of Memory, attached to which is a rather sad tale—but more of that later. Compton Acres appears the work of a collector gone mad; an enthusiast who refused to stop at stamps or beer mats, having rather

more grandiose notions. Stylistically, it seems to have fallen out of favour with many garden designers, who have a preference for an overall theme that is appropriate to the landscape. As an outsider, it was a revelation to me to find so much controversy and (ahem) *differing* opinions within the gardening fraternity. Surely if every garden was identical, then your average visitor would soon be bored silly. Compton Acres is obviously representative of a certain era, with its own concepts about style. Of course, it would be all very well if the gardens stood for just a moment in our horticultural history, but they are far more than that.

It's simple, people love these gardens. On a research visit to another garden (not eventually included in this project) I was practically restrained physically by two women, desperate to tell me that I should see Compton Acres. Visitors genuinely enjoy the diversity of these gardens.

The Italian Garden is perhaps the most photographed and renowned of Compton's various horticultural 'rooms'. Peter Thoday describes it, along with the Japanese Garden, as one of two 'jokers in the pack', in that it is a foreign garden within a very English seaside setting. Although he remarks on how difficult it can be to find the plants to echo a Mediterranean style, he believes that visitors appreciate 'the overall spectacle of the garden.' In fact, director Stanley Kubrick admired the symmetry and elegance of the Italian Garden so much that he used it as a location for his film 'Barry Lyndon'. And with the recent addition of an Italianate villa, it's easy to forget that you are in Dorset—especially when the sun's shining.

A description of every single garden at Compton would probably entail its own book, but it seems remiss not to mention, for instance, the Wooded Valley; its massive rhododendrons, in spring gloriously colourful, but always enveloping, shielding the visitor from the frenetic outside world. The Garden of Memory was built in remembrance of the children of J. S. Beard, who saved Compton from dereliction after the Second World War—the three died tragically young, a reminder that death, as well as life, is a story that every garden can tell.

And as for life, well the gardens teem with it—from the birds and the bees to the more unexpected. Koi carp and terrapins are curiously satisfying to watch as they go about their daily business (which for the terrapins involves doing, well, not much really), and if you're very fortunate you might catch a glimpse of the rare sand lizards that lounge in the secluded crevices of the Heather Garden. With so much to discover, what are you doing just reading this?!

The Good, the Bad & the Ugly

Compton Acres is blessed with an array of wildlife, but generally it is the likes of the birds and the badgers that get the good press. Do they just have better PR, or is the insect invasion really a threat to gardens everywhere?

The good...centipedes

You'd think with all those legs they'd get round the garden in no time, munching on prize plants as they go. Actually, they only occasionally feast on the greenery, in times of drought for instance, preferring the taste of insect flesh—like the Hannibal Lectors of the creepy crawly world, they'll devour most bugs from snails and slugs to vine weevils.

The bad...sawflies

These rather attractive looking green and yellow bugs are the stuff of nightmares for gardeners. Their modus operandi involves drilling into the foliage of plants with a saw-toothed tube (hence their name) with which they lay their eggs. Once the eggs hatch, the larvae eat their way outwards, quickly reducing leaves to mere skeletons. Frightening, eh?

The ugly...leatherjackets

Yuk...these huge, super-squishy, brown grubs are actually the larvae of the harmless Daddy Longlegs (Crane Fly). These are so ugly, they even revolt each other.* They also smell and have no table manners. ** Oh, and they're a pest in the garden too—feeding on the roots of plants.

(*author's right to supposition)
(**more of the same, author possibly pathological liar)

Highlights

The Japanese Garden

With its re-creation of far-flung, exotic beauty, this seems the most quirky of the gardens. As Peter explains, 'oriental gardens are a completely different art form.' This stunning garden works due to the attention to detail. Simpson was very careful to bring in genuine Japanese artefacts, coupled with Japanese expertise, to ensure that the area had the right feel. Enfolded within the landform and surrounded with dense trees, crucially all reminders of its true setting aren't allowed to distract the visitor.

The Red-Eared Terrapins

A bemused crowd regards the terrapins basking in the sun in the Rock and Water Garden. It isn't until one of them deigns to slowly, leisurely stretch a leg that the onlookers realise that they are, in fact, real. No, these seemingly monumentally lazy creatures are not plastic. I suspect when the crowd turns its collective back the terrapins perform acrobatic stunts and amuse each other with graceful pirouettes and... break dancing (they'd be great at that, wouldn't they?). Now that really would be a highlight.

The Koi Carp

The carp at Compton are HUGE! Swimming shark-like with their dorsal fins above water, belly flopping recklessly onto lily pads after pellets of fish food, probably eating those unfortunates who happen to trip and fall from the stepping stones of the Japanese Garden...

Compton Acres, 164 Canford Cliffs Road, Poole, Dorset, BH13 7ES, 01202 700778
www.comptonacres.co.uk

STOURTON HOUSE FLOWER GARDEN

Stourton, Wiltshire

Abundant   Understated   Fertile   Endearing   Tenacious

What was immediately striking about Stourton House was the atmosphere of a garden time forgot. With the spectre of the hugely popular National Trust's Stourhead looming over it, this smaller garden appears to be the underdog. As I sat talking to owner Elizabeth Bullivant, several customers stopped to sheepishly enquire the way to the tearooms. Exhausted by Stourhead's gardens, suffering from garden fatigue and an overload of beauteous vistas, all they wanted was to scoff cream teas.

Whilst I'm not one to knock the spiritual and restorative benefits of a cream tea, it's impossible not to feel saddened that this garden rarely receives the attention it deserves. It was not always so. The garden has featured several times on television programmes, such as the BBC's 'Gardeners' World', and Elisabeth is a leading authority on drying flowers,

having also written books on the subject.

She still does a small amount of picking and drying her shrubs and herbaceous flowers, producing beautiful bouquets which are available for purchase, and happily, dried flowers do seem to be making a comeback. However, sharing a car park with one of the National Trust's finest doesn't do her garden any favours; it is not unknown for coach parties aiming for the flower garden to mistakenly end up at Stourhead purely by accident (and perhaps partly due to the larger, more impressive sign, though this is one of those occasions when it should be remembered that bigger doesn't necessarily mean better).

It's such a shame, because Elizabeth's flower garden has so much to offer. Excitingly, it has a real sense of discovery about it—and there's plenty here that you are unlikely to see elsewhere. Gardening is always a battle to bend nature to suit the gardener's will, and sometimes at Stourton House it looks like Elizabeth is losing the fight. Could this be a garden in the process of being reclaimed by nature?

It is certainly the case that Tarzan wouldn't look out of place swinging from the trees in the woodland, and in the 'secret garden' area I fully expected to discover new tribes of people when wandering lost in its midst (unlikely in Wiltshire?). Appearances, however, are as deceptive as ever. Elizabeth strongly repudiates the idea that this is a garden in which nature has the upper hand, pointing instead to Stourton House's modern naturalistic ethos.

Elizabeth explains that hers is a 'very unorthodox' garden, she likes it to 'enjoy itself' and chooses to 'plant things where we think they'd like to grow.' Plants are allowed to mature, so the visitor can see immense rhododendrons and a profusion of hydrangeas in their full glory.

Yet you never quite know what you might find in the undergrowth; all sorts of curiosities are concealed in the nooks and crannies of this garden. Take one winding path through the woodland area and you might see rare camellias

with two colours on the same bush or flowers half one colour and half another; delve deeper and watch out for smatterings of distinctive chequered snake's head fritillaries. You may well be dazzled by the blaze of colour produced by the spring performance of scented rhododendrons, azaleas, magnolias and camellias, but don't forget to look down as you could well miss more subtle delights such as erythroniums. These striking plants, with graceful lily-like flowers and decorative foliage, are relatively unknown in the UK. Most species have North American origins and both 'White Beauty' and the aptly named 'Pagoda' varieties thrive in the shady, moist conditions of Stourton House's woodland.

Elizabeth is endlessly knowledgeable about her garden, seemingly familiar with every inch of it, and conversant with the hiding place of every unusual flower, down to the smallest violet. Her horticultural anecdotes are not only informative, they make a visit to Stourton House all the more personal.

Her pride in the garden is obvious when she describes how, in the drought of summer 1976, her lawn remained green whilst those of other gardens were rendered brown and patchy. Her lawn thrived because it has a high ratio of natural plants (such as clover) to grass—another example of how Elizabeth works with her natural environment to get the results she wants. Buttercups and daisies are also allowed to adorn the lawn—and when they do, to the delight of visitors, it is Elizabeth's policy not to mow the grass. In deed, she actively encourages the growth of wildflowers and her garden is full of very rare wild species.

Teasel is one of her favourites. Again this plant proved its worth during the hot summer of 1976 when everything else was dying. The leaves form a sort of cup structure, collecting water for bees, birds and any creature with a serious thirst in the morning.

A savaged great mullein was another she pointed out—strange I thought, surely a gardener wouldn't draw attention to a plant that was obviously the horticultural version of MacDonald's. It turns out this is precisely why she has it in her garden; the caterpillars love it and thus her cultivated plants are left un-assaulted. Ideal!

Stourton Flower Garden was created and nurtured by a husband and wife; and some might feel that the sense of loss is palpable as Elizabeth struggles on without Anthony, forever reminded of him by the endeavours that surround her. She, however, is having none of this sentimental rubbish, busy instead with plans for new areas—including a bog garden—and safe in the knowledge that a past ancestor reportedly reached the astonishing age of 149! She seems an unstoppable force, her enthusiasm for Stourton House unrelenting. All she needs you to do, however, is to walk though her gate. It is likely that huge estates like Stourhead will be maintained by trusts for the future, but gardens like Elizabeth's, with such a personal atmosphere, also need our support. This is a true plant lovers' garden—let it be your next discovery.

Flower Power

At Stourton Flower Garden they use flower petals in a number of cake recipes. Many flowers are edible; here're a few you might want to try.

Marigolds and violets can add interest to salads or be used to garnish dishes. Nasturtiums are also an ideal addition to salads. Not only do they look sensational, but they have a slightly peppery tang which really enhances flavour, especially when combined with watercress and rocket.

Rose petals are great in jams, sugars, syrups, jellies and teas.

The Tiger lily has long been a component of Chinese cooking. The striking orange petals can be cooked, then used to stuff fish.

Always take care over the flowers you choose to chomp on. Remember, some may be poisonous, or treated with pesticides, plus pinching them from your neighbour's garden is likely to result in an ASBO.

Highlights

The Daffodils

Elizabeth specialises in these cheerful harbingers of spring (forever tainted by the irritating Wordsworth). March and April are the best time to see many rare and RHS prize-winning varieties. Look out for Lizzie Bee and Busy Liz, daffodils bred by Elizabeth herself. Lemon Curd Cream is a favourite with its characteristic lemon yellow split trumphet. This tasty-sounding daff is named after a delicious cake that Elizabeth's daughter Caroline bakes. Don't forget to try its namesake at the tearooms!

The Hydrangeas

Every year a spectacular Hydrangea gala is held at the picturesque Stourton village church, with over 1,000 flowers from the garden on display. Stourton House is renowned for its cultivation of Hydrangeas, with 270 types—some developed in the garden itself. One, a huge *Hydrangea verlosa*, is now to be called 'Anthony Bullivant' in honour of her husband and never fails to impress both visitors and top horticulturalists.

Biennial Thistle

Just because I love its Latin name, *Silybum*, and love even more Elizabeth's relish in showing it off to her visitors (despite her many rare and exotic cultivated plants).

If someone makes you the gift of a plant—be rude and don't bother thanking them for it. According to folklore a thank you will guarantee the death of the plant. (Of course, according to polite society, no gratitude will guarantee no more presents.)

Stourton House Flower Garden, Stourton, Nr Warminster, Wiltshire, BA12 6QF,
01747 840417

ABBEY HOUSE GARDENS

Malmesbury, Wiltshire

Irreverent   Vivacious   Humorous   Triumphant   Intriguing

It seems incongruous for a garden, often a Mecca of rural tranquillity, to be the centre of a bustling market town. Yet Abbey House Gardens so perfectly complement Malmesbury, a historic town in the Cotswolds dominated by the towering presence of the ruins of an ancient abbey. Like the town, this garden is not always a peaceful place to be—it has far too much going on for that.

From the moment Barbara Pollard sashayed along the path to meet us, resplendent in the tiniest of shorts (which I'd love to have the figure to wear myself), heart-patterned pink and white wellies, and multicoloured hair and nails, it was obvious this was a garden like no other. What has become so compelling over the year of filming in a wide range of gardens is how well they reflect the personalities of their creators; Abbey House is no exception. Witty, irreverent, and bursting with joyous colour and energy, this is a garden that sticks two fingers up at the horticultural orthodoxy. 'They (garden designers) say it's busy, so so busy,' Ian Pollard tells us with just a trace of anger in his voice, 'but unfortunately that's what people tend to like; certainly we do—we won't have any of that minimalism crap!'

When the couple and their children moved to Abbey House twelve years ago, they had no intention of opening the gardens to the public—which was lucky really, as a quick examination of photographs from the time shows an untidy field rather than a garden. After Malmesbury town's proposal for a millennium celebration was thrown out because the government was already set on building the ill-fated, and frankly rubbish, Millennium Dome, a disappointed Ian, who had been chairman of the project, came up with a new idea. He felt Malmesbury, as a small market town, was in trouble—it needed something to lure people away from the superstores and back to the high street. So he decided to plant 2,000 roses to celebrate year 2,000 and to open the garden to the public. And the rest, as they say, is history.

In just ten years, Abbey House has been transformed

by the hard work and vision of Ian and Barbara into an exuberant Eden, with a larger collection of plants and shrubs than in many botanical gardens. Abbey House isn't afraid to think big, and, as the colours just keep on coming, it's tempting to think there's something a little bit cheeky, even slightly audacious, about achievement on this scale. The Royal Horticultural Society certainly seems to think

so. Ian reveals that the editor of the RHS magazine has had 'three articles presented to him on this garden; he's refused all three of them on the basis that you can't make a good garden in less than twenty years.' Hmm, well maybe most of the population couldn't, but the evidence is undisputable—and most of the visiting public seem to be wholly won over by the Abbey House's charms.

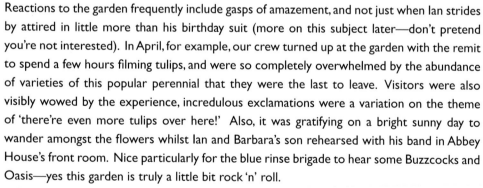

Reactions to the garden frequently include gasps of amazement, and not just when Ian strides by attired in little more than his birthday suit (more on this subject later—don't pretend you're not interested). In April, for example, our crew turned up at the garden with the remit to spend a few hours filming tulips, and were so completely overwhelmed by the abundance of varieties of this popular perennial that they were the last to leave. Visitors were also visibly wowed by the experience, incredulous exclamations were a variation on the theme of 'there're even more tulips over here!' Also, it was gratifying on a bright sunny day to wander amongst the flowers whilst Ian and Barbara's son rehearsed with his band in Abbey House's front room. Nice particularly for the blue rinse brigade to hear some Buzzcocks and Oasis—yes this garden is truly a little bit rock 'n' roll.

In spite of the lighthearted atmosphere, it is transparently obvious that it takes a lot of time and effort to create, and then maintain, a garden like Abbey House. Ian made his money from property development and used to run his company from Hazelbury Manor, which required eight gardeners to keep its grounds in order. Ian explains that he felt 'the gardeners had a better lifestyle' than his own, and this was the impetus behind his rather radical career change. Ian admits that gardening is not without its stresses however; a reoccurring thought being, 'Oh God, what's dropped off, fallen over, or being attacked today?'

What makes the garden really special for many people is its sympathetic blend of the ancient and the contemporary. Benedictine monks once gardened at the site and this influenced Ian to design a medieval-style garden, fashioned using formal structures and a rich palette of colours. It's easy to imagine monks demurely strolling along the yew-hedged walkways; a sense emphasised by a statue of a resting monk in the Lady Chapel area of the garden. A clock-shaped herb garden (originally a response to a play on words: planting time vs. thyme) with raised beds containing approximately 1200 herbs with medicinal or culinary properties is based on the principles espoused in a 9th-century poem. Enclosed in a circular colonnade (itself a framework for entwined vines of apples, pears, peaches, medlars, quinces and grapes) and with a fountain as a centrepiece, this is a restful place to sit—a lightly scented retreat from the bright frivolity of the other formal gardens.

The abbey itself was founded in 676 AD by Aldhelm, who had received his religious tutelage nearby from the Celtic Benedictine monk Maidulph. Ian has recorded this at Abbey House with a Celtic Cross Knot Garden—'a real pain in the arse to keep in shape'. On the borders on either side of the garden a Celtic scroll has been planted, and its meaning 'everlasting' or going forever forward but looking forever back seems the ideal epitaph for Abbey House.

Next to the belvedere, a beautiful location with rather daunting tree-top views over the river, and perfect for picnicking is the Stew Pond. This is a reminder that the ever practical monks often had 'stew ponds' near their kitchens to keep fish ready for Friday's stew. These days, however, refreshments are available at the garden, including juices made from its own fruit, so no fishing!

The Pollards are keen to explain that the garden is more than a mere period piece, a re-creation of one moment in time. Instead, the design strives to evoke resonances from the garden's past, to conjure up a feeling of a long-gone era. They haven't allowed themselves to be restrained by the considerable history of the area; the formality is interspersed with plenty of quirky touches. A face carved into the yew hedge, a water sculpture by Barry Mason (which creates an optical illusion and cries out to be touched with its sleek, smooth contours and its cool flowing water), and some truly spooky statues—this is a garden where you must look, then look again.

And there are yet more surprises in store. On the other side of the house is a completely different world, with regards to gardens anyway (what do you think this is, Lord of the Rings?). Pathways traverse the steep slope behind the house, dropping down to the river, and all of a sudden the ambience alters. This area is wild, naturalistic, and in complete contrast to the gardens above. Soothing and serene, how curious it is to remember that this garden is in the midst of a busy market town?

Unmissable in this part of the garden is a simply huge tree fern, which is so old it would have been around about the same time that Captain Cook landed on Botany Bay. If only they could talk, eh? Although I expect its chief concern would be why it had been dragged all the way from Tasmania to Wiltshire.

Another gorgeous feature is a waterfall which, surrounded as it is by maples and azaleas, reflects Ian and Barbara's interest in Japanese mythology. The cascade falls onto a 'fishstone' and represents the fish's struggles to swim upwards—on reaching the top it transforms into a dragon, symbolic of good fortune. It is a parable of humankind's efforts to achieve and attain, which, the Pollards note, is extremely appropriate with regards to Abbey House. However, when Ian saw the original waterfall, the inspiration for his own, he found it was half the size! For me, this is what Abbey House is all about: they just can't help being brazenly bigger and better than the majority of gardens across the UK.

© Abbey House Gardens, 2007

© Abbey House Gardens, 2007

Highlights

Shock Horror!

There's a naked man in the garden! It's very entertaining to watch visitors' reactions to Ian, as he works away in the garden in little more than a leopard print thong and a pair of wellies. There are a few mutterings from men along the lines of, 'What's wrong with wearing a pair of shorts?', but on the whole everyone responds admirably. The ladies do tend to avert their eyes as they walk by though, and then quickly turn back to surreptitiously take photos of his bum. Both Barbara and Ian love to garden naked, although they do cover up slightly when the public are admitted. The garden does host 'Clothing Optional' days if you fancy going *au natural* yourself.

Garden of Dreams

This was taken literally by some, when during a performance of a play in the garden, several elderly visitors fell into a deep sleep—and there was considerable difficulty in arousing them from their torpor. And no, it wasn't because they were watching yet another unfunny Shakespeare comedy; they were under the influence of nearby hallucinogenic *Brugmansia* plants. I don't know, imbibing druggy fumes in broad daylight...it's a slippery slope!

Abbey House Gardens, Malmesbury, Wiltshire, SN16 9AS, 01666 822212
www.abbeyhousegardens.co.uk

WESTONBIRT, THE NATIONAL ARBORETUM

Tetbury, Gloucestershire

Diverse   Educational   Eventful   Magical   Colourful

It was the vision of Robert Holford, who planted his very first trees in the arboretum in 1829, which was instrumental in building Westonbirt's reputation today as home to many of the world's most exotic trees and shrubs. For the last fifty years however, the arboretum has been carefully nurtured by the Forestry Commission. Under their guidance, Westonbirt has become not only an ornamental collection of trees and shrubs, but a scientific one: a living laboratory dedicated to conservation, research and education.

Curator of Westonbirt, Simon Toomer, tall, thin, upright and strangely tree-like himself, describes the arboretum as a botanical garden for trees. He believes Westonbirt's enduring appeal lies in its picturesque-style layout. Holford's love of art and design led him to plant trees in a manner which would be pleasing to the eye—rather than species by species, which was the fashion in horticultural circles at the time.

This, of course, is the most remarkable aspect of Holford's endeavours. It takes real imagination to envisage how the trees will look when mature—something that would not happen in Holford's lifetime. He was meticulous in his design, even flattening a road and moving Westonbirt village so as to get a perfect vista along the main drive from his house to the end of his land.

Meticulous is a word that also recurs often in Simon Toomer's vocabulary. He explains that Westonbirt is committed to research; from a seed in a propagating unit, to a sapling, and onwards, they keep extensive records. Impressively, he reiterates that very few plants are brought in from other botanical collections or from garden centres, as Westonbirt have their own full-time propagator on site and have their own seed collecting expeditions.

> **"Westonbirt is magical because Holford had dual passions for art and botanicals and skilfully combined the two."**
> Simon Toomer, curator at Westonbirt, The National Arboretum

With eight people on his Tree Team, Simon's job is to ensure that the trees are healthy, to advise on any remedial work necessary, and to maintain the original picturesque-influenced layout of the site. This means a certain amount of tree removal, earning the mild-mannered curator the appellation of 'The Toominator', according to one Westonbirt employee. Hacking down trees (Simon corrects me here with the much less dramatic 'felling') may be upsetting for some. However, it's easy to forget that trees, as living beings, do eventually reach the end of their lives; they need to be cut down for safety reasons, or to allow surrounding trees the chance to thrive.

Accompanied everywhere by a tiny Jack Russell, Twig, the Tree Team clearly loves its work. It's impressive to watch, fit young men shimmying nimbly up trees with chainsaws banging precariously around their thighs. An enormous amount of work goes into the upkeep of Westonbirt, so I think it's very important to truly appreciate it. Plus defiant dog Twig, hindering progress by using the ropes and equipment as her own personal adventure playground, always made me smile.

According to The Toominator, what 'does it for him' is the need for imagination in his work. The ability to conceptualise how an area will look in the far future as a result of his plans and alterations is all important. Despite the emphasis on detailed records and research, Westonbirt still holds the odd surprise for Simon. He does occasionally bump into plants he wasn't expecting, and he describes the excitement in seeing new introductions bloom for the first time. I'm sure it's so, but for me as an ex tomboy the tree climbing seemed much more appealing.

The National Arboretum, Westonbirt really is an enchanted wood filled with glorious sights for the visitor to feast upon: the world renowned display of autumn colour, the eclectic and sometimes charmingly eccentric programme of events...and the unexpected attraction of the Tree Team's posteriors. There is definitely a reason for everyone to enjoy Westonbirt, and anyone who claims there isn't, certainly hasn't seen the Tree Team in action!

Nevertheless, the words 'wet', 'uncomfortable' and 'lost' describe my first encounter with Westonbirt; with 600 acres to traverse, the right clothing and footwear is essential. Twisting the well known phrase 'can't see the trees for the wood' seems remarkably apt—it is easy to wander bewildered around a large arboretum without really 'seeing' anything. Westonbirt, however, excels at finding new ways to make visitors look closer at their surroundings. Various trails are marked out throughout the seasons emphasising which trees and shrubs are at their optimum. Healing trails describe the various medicinal uses of trees and shrubs, and there are numerous opportunities to learn about the diverse wildlife (birds, bats and badgers just to name a few, and practice my alliteration) that inhabit the arboretum. I was fortunate enough to witness some fox cubs play fighting in the early evening—and right by one of the pathways too. Also, there are a multitude of events throughout the year aimed at children, with Westonbirt providing a unique outdoor classroom.

To truly enjoy the arboretum then, it is crucial not to blaze along the pathways but to take the time to stop and really examine the trees around you. For the film that this book accompanies, we spent a day (covering a ridiculously small amount of the arboretum) gathering footage of bark, leaves and boughs. The variation of texture and shade in bark was staggering; all of a sudden it was exciting to run ahead and find a tree that was much more unusual than the last. Maple trees are known for their vividly coloured leaves, but some also have very bizarre bark. My favourite is the Snake-bark maple (*Acer hersii*) with its sinister green snakeskin trunk, and also the Paper-bark maple (*Acer griseum*) which produces an interesting tattered effect—difficult to resist the urge to peel it though. Maples are not to be missed at Westonbirt,

especially when they go crazy with colour in the autumn.

Basically, Westonbirt is split into the Old Arboretum containing Holford's aesthetically pleasing tree-lined drives and an array of rare and ancient specimen trees, and Silk Wood, home to many more native trees and a wilder affair altogether.

Silk Wood is also home to the National Japanese Maple Collection including almost 500 forms of this diverse and much loved species. Volunteers from the 'Friends of Westonbirt Arboretum', a 20,000-strong organisation dedicated to the site, assisted in the planting and maintaining of the collection, which was newly laid out in 2005.

What is clear when speaking to any of the 'Friends' is the enthusiasm and affection that they have for Westonbirt—I've not seen anything like it anywhere else! Just as each tree, in its long-lived nature, has a story, each 'Friend' has a favourite tree or a personal attachment to a part of Westonbirt. Some even 'adopt' a tree—one volunteer did so as a valentine present for his lover. Who said getting damp feet and aching legs in a huge forest couldn't be romantic?

> **"God almighty first planted a garden...and indeed it is the purest of human pleasures..."**
> Francis Bacon
> Robert Holford marked this passage in his copy of Bacon's essays.

It would be near on impossible to get across the scale and grandeur of Westonbirt in writing. So I'm not going to attempt to describe the different areas of Westonbirt (why not go yourself and pick up a map from the info centre!) but rather some of the reasons that make it more than just a great walk in the woods.

Firstly, well...it's a great walk in the woods! I don't think this should be undervalued, there are fewer and fewer places to enjoy the countryside and some tranquillity away from modernity, and Westonbirt really is a perfect place to stretch your legs—fitness for you, but also fitness for your dog (if you have one) as Silk Wood is heavenly for hairy tearaways on the rampage. The Forestry Commission is keen to encourage visitors to think of Westonbirt as one giant health tonic. Tai Chi classes, calorie counting walks, well-being weekends (complete with meditation and reflexology classes) have all been available at Westonbirt—it's worth checking out their website to see what new suggestions they have for persuading people to get off their fat lardy arses. Not that anyone at Westonbirt appears to be particularly lardy, probably due to the likelihood of getting lost in Silk Wood for a week and having to survive on nuts, berries, dogs et cetera (no I'm joking really, no sense of direction is my own debilitating problem, that and being rubbish at reading a map; and I'd never eat a dog, I couldn't manage a whole one, thanks).

When you're bored of endless fresh air, there are always the annual concerts in the summer—in the fresh air! Providing it doesn't pour down, and if it does be British and

get over it, then these really are fun—Westonbirt makes a splendid alternative venue to listen to live music. Pop, rock, classical, the programme at Westonbirt is varied so there's likely to be something to suit your tastes, unless you're hugely into French hip hop, which probably wouldn't be catered for. Myself, I went to a classical concert, the trees providing a superior and imposing setting for the music and end of night fireworks. However, these can be quite posh affairs, so don't forget your fold-away table and chairs. And your sense of patriotism.

Westonbirt is a place for all seasons. If you visit only for the drama of autumn, you'll miss the subtle charm of spring and summer and the stark beauty of winter, with its ghostlike atmosphere and skeletal trees. It is both a home for the ancient, at least one tree in the Silk Wood, a Small-leaved Lime (*Tilla cordata*) is believed to be over 2000 years old, and for the future, in its constant work with seed propagation and conservation of endangered species. Just to look briefly at some of the uses of trees and wood— timber, paper, furniture, rubber, pharmaceuticals, alcohol and medicines to name a few—is a reminder that you should support the arboretum with your visits. Westonbirt: the mysterious world of the tree revealed!

Painswick Rococo Garden, Painswick, Gloucestershire, GL6 6TH, 01452 813204
www.rococogarden.co.uk

BOURTON HOUSE GARDEN

Bourton-on-the-Hill, Gloucestershire

Eccentric   Vivid   Artistic   Precise   Compact

Faced with the ultimate difficult (and rather vague) question, owner of Bourton House, Monique Paice, responds with, 'What can I say the garden's about? It's about serenity, tranquillity, a great feeling of accomplishment for all of us here.' When the Canadian ex fashion designer first bought the property she found 'a palette with which she could play'. Her use of a painting metaphor is revealing, as this compact three-acre garden, which juxtaposes formality with contemporary flair, is simply bursting with colours and texture. The gardens provide the ideal setting for Bourton House, a typical example of a Cotswolds manor, its classicism reflected by the combination of precise and imaginative topiary and the colourful herbaceous borders surrounding the main lawn.

Monique comments that visitors to the garden are often 'totally surprised by what they find'. Many of them are obviously hooked on Bourton's charms, 'we get a lot of repeat visitors; a lot of people have been coming for years, and it's lovely to recognise old friends.' So what is it about Bourton House Garden that's so special? Perhaps it is because it so clearly reflects the people who have created it, those who work every day to keep it looking at its optimum. It is not an example of a large impersonal garden, with style and content strictly defined by its history, where it can be hard sometimes to imagine or hear the voices of the people behind it—instead it is infused with the characters of those who love to work and create within its boundaries.

Monique is determined that visitors realise that the garden is a team effort. She relies on the horticultural knowledge of head gardener Paul Nicholls and his partner in crime,

Jackie Rae. 'They are the more physical side of the team, and I pretend I'm the more cerebral side,' she explains with a laugh, 'but I bow to their superior knowledge when it comes to plant names and all the rest. I do know how to point at something and say I like it or I don't.' Head gardener Paul admits that knowing Monique's horticultural preferences is 'the key to the relationship', but he is also able to add his own creative input. 'That's why it's interesting working here at Bourton…you can express yourself somewhat…in a lot of big gardens you can't do that.' Jackie is very quick to pinpoint Monique's dislikes, 'Pink, she doesn't like anything pink.' Monique concurs admitting that, 'if it's pink it hasn't got much chance of surviving here', which sounds rather brutal! Instead, she prefers 'strong looking plants' and places an emphasis on structure in the garden, 'I like shapes, or plants with a lot of texture and shape to them…You need architecture in the garden and the most changeable architecture you've got is in your plants, because you're always doing something to them—letting them grow or cutting them back or clipping them. You need that shape… For me design in the garden needs to see repetition of shapes…not necessarily colours. Colours are a very difficult thing to put your hand on, I feel, because people see them very differently. If one colour works in the garden consistently it's the colour green.'

So green is in and pink is out, although there is no lack of colour in Bourton's flamboyant wide and abundant herbaceous borders. But this is a garden where the plants are allowed to reveal the beauty of their design, where the eye is drawn to their unique structures—Bourton never relies on the mere prettiness of its flowers. In fact, the most obvious emblem of the English country garden is rarely to be found here—Monique has no love of rose gardens and will only use roses as part of a scheme.

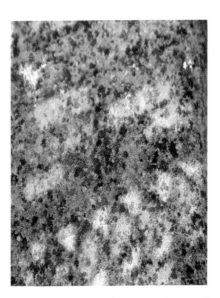

One shape that recurs—in the hedges, the ironwork, the benches—is that of the ogee. The ogee is a shape consisting of a concave arc that flows into a convex arc to form an S-shaped curve with vertical ends. Its origins are Arabic and it was introduced in the 14th century, quickly becoming popular in medieval England and also in Venice, Italy, resulting in its other well known moniker, the Venetian Arch. In 'The Analysis of Beauty' published in 1753, the English painter and engraver William Hogarth referred to the ogee as the 'line of beauty' espousing the belief that it was inherent in all successful visual art. So it's no surprise to find it here at Bourton House, in a garden so deliberately designed and laid out. Surprisingly, however, Monique does seem to have missed something—I did encounter a few pink flowers. I shouldn't have mentioned it; their days will be numbered.

Monique notes that visitors are first impressed by the 'extraordinary' tithe barn, which they walk through to reach the garden. The barn was built in 1570 by Richard Palmer. With its sloping floors and massive beams, the barn is certainly atmospheric; it makes the ideal setting for regular art exhibitions. The Brewhouse in the courtyard is from the same era; a romantic Cotswold idyll, it has made appearances in magazines including 'Hello' and is regarded as one of the best cottages for honeymooning couples.

Bourton House itself was rebuilt on the foundation of Palmer's Tudor manor in the early 18th century. The current owners describe its past as 'chequered'; what that means I don't know, but people appear to have been in a hurry to leave—the house has had seven lots of owners in the last fifty years. Perhaps the house exerts an evil influence over its inhabitants compelling them to perform murderous acts—or maybe past owners have simply been repelled by the amount of work necessary to maintain a property of Bourton's size and age. The Paices, however, fell in love with its dilapidated charm when they first saw it in 1983, and have enthusiastically thrown themselves into its renovation. The grounds had retained some original features, such as a kitchen garden and an 18th-century raised walk, but were severely neglected. Weeds such as nettles and bindweed had taken over and everything was, well, a rampant overgrown mess.

Twenty years on and the garden is about as immaculate as it is possible for any garden to be. Proving rather unnecessary in the modern world, the kitchen garden was re-styled into a more manageable potager—which is a source of many fresh ingredients used in the delicious lunches Bourton House offers. The raised walk inspired Monique to get out her sketchbook and design the staircase accompanied by a series of profusely planted terraces, whilst a visit to a friend in Canada encouraged her to construct the unusual shade house, which offers a little extra protection to tender plants.

"Garden: One of a vast number of free outdoor restaurants operated by charity-minded amateurs in an effort to provide healthful, balanced meals for insects, birds and animals."
A useful definition from Henry Beard and Roy McKie, 'Gardener's Dictionary'

The fortuitous discovery of a natural spring has allowed the important presence of water in the garden—in the form of fountains, ponds and plunge pools. Deep herbaceous borders, one for tender plants and one for sub-tropical varieties, provide more than enough delights for the keen plantsman or woman throughout the seasons.

Jackie's particular niche is propagation and glasshouse work. She also takes care of the succulents, which in the summer provide a fine display of bizarre shapes and textures whilst soaking up the sun in raised alpine beds. In addition, there is a seven-acre plantation of a wide range of trees opposite the garden—this area also plays host to captivating sculptures such as Andrew Darke's 'Cleaved Air', a very simple piece, its beauty in the movement it makes when touched by even the faintest breeze.

'My expectations have always been for perfection,' Monique explains, and at Bourton House that message certainly shines through.

Terrifying Topiary

The horror, the horror! Wait a minute, why the hysteria? Head gardener Paul elucidates on his relationship with topiary, 'Me and topiary…here's a good tip for someone setting a garden out—don't have any hedges, don't have any topiary work,' he continues with a laugh, 'perhaps don't have any plants.' He admits that Bourton House has 'quite a name' for its topiary, and if he and the other gardeners sometimes wished there was a little less of it, then it seems they have Monique's husband, Richard, to blame.

Monique explains, 'If we've got all that box to clip it's thanks to him. He was born in the wrong century; should have been around in the 17th, 18th [century], when there were masses of people clipping away happily. In the 21st century it's not the smartest thing to do.' The demands of modern life often require that gardens are designed in a way that allows them to be low maintenance.

Topiary has its origins in ancient Roman times. The Romans adored formal gardens and employed a special slave—known by the Latin as a *topiarius*—to look after the ornamental topia, a word derived from the Greek for 'places'. It is speculated that Greek, Egyptian or Jewish slaves were responsible for introducing the art of topiary to the Romans. After the fall of the Roman Empire, Italian monks continued to create topiary in the cloisters of their monasteries. In this way, knowledge of the art was retained, allowing it to become wildly popular during the Middle Ages and the Renaissance, with proponents producing everything from elaborate colonnades to donkeys and sailing boats. By 1520 the French had joined the party culminating in the grand designs of Andre Le Notre for King Louis the Fourteenth at the Palace of Versailles.

Late as ever, topiary didn't reach its zenith in England until the 17th century. It was a relatively short-lived craze. Capability Brown's ideas for landscaped gardening quickly became the new mania and various critics poured scorn on the quirky art. Alexander Pope famously drove the knife in, killing off the fashion for clipped shapes in his satirical essay entitled 'Verdant Sculpture', which was published by 'The Guardian' in 1713.

In it he catalogued mocking descriptions of topiary specimens such as, 'Adam and Eve in yew; Adam a little shattered by the fall of the tree of knowledge in the great storm; Eve and the serpent very flourishing...The tower of Babel, not yet finished...St George in box; his arm scarce long enough, but will be in condition to stick the dragon by next April,' and 'A quickset

hog, shot up into a porcupine, by its being forgot a week in rainy weather.'

Luckily, topiary never completely died out; examples could still be found in some of England's more eccentric gardens. The Victorians revived the art and it seems that today, despite the work needed to maintain it, topiary is thriving. To date everything from sumo wrestlers to dinosaurs have been topiarised.

Nothing so silly at Bourton, however; here topiary is used to give the garden a strong design, to add structure, to give a sense of control—a good idea in today's unbalanced, topsy-turvy world. Along with the crisp lines of the Knot Garden and the Parterre, geometric shapes of box abound— pyramids, spirals, cones and ogees. Both Jackie and Paul describe a sense of accomplishment when they see the smartness of the newly clipped hedges. Due to time constraints they only clip once a year, usually in late August. We wondered why Paul kept dipping his shears in a bucket of water whilst clipping and he explained, 'I work that fast and that hard, those shear tips get really red hot and that's to cool them down because I don't want to burn the box.' Gardening humour aside, the real reason is a useful tip for anyone considering topiary or hedges in their own garden. Both box and yew contain a very sticky sap which collects on the shears and sticks the blades together, making cutting much more difficult. Paul suggests either using the aforementioned bucket to keep cleaning the shears or clipping following rain.

Topiary is transparently a challenging facet of gardening design. Paul comments, 'We fairly well enjoy doing it', which doesn't sound wildly enthusiastic, but maybe hints that this is an art which requires a huge amount of patience and some skill. Nevertheless the effort has paid off at Bourton; its living architecture provides the garden with a perfect, and pleasingly individual, backdrop.

Best Ever Fruit Cake

Ingredients

850 g plain flour	3 tsp baking powder
680 g margarine	450 g pecans
565 g sugar	450 g golden raisins
10 eggs	280 g glace pineapple
2 tbsp lemon flavouring	450 g traffic glace cherries
1 tsp salt	340 g candied peel
425 g white marzipan	

For the Florentine Topping:

110 g skinned hazelnuts	110 g blanched almonds
170 g brazil nuts	170 g flaked almonds
280 g glace cherries	225 g golden syrup

Cover raisins with hot water and set aside. Cut up all fruit and dredge in ½ cup of flour. Cream the butter and sugar. Add the eggs one at a time, then the lemon flavouring. Next add the dry ingredients, and stir the fruit into the batter. Line a 30 cm x 30 cm square pan, divided into four cakes or two 20 cm square tins. Bake covered with silicone paper at 300 °F, 160 °C or gas mark 2 for 2 or more hours. Place a pan of water in the bottom of the oven to keep the cakes from drying out.

Reserve 225 g of the cake batter. Add these ingredients, at the time of putting the cake into bake. After the cake has cooked 1¼ hours, add the topping and bake a further 40 minutes covered, then another 10/15 minutes for the nuts to colour.

Wrap and store for at least 4 weeks.

Roasted Parsnip & Parmesan Soup

Ingredients

450 g parsnips cut into lengths	1 tbsp plain flour
50 g freshly grated parmesan cheese	1.5 litres vegetable stock
1 tbsp olive oil	salt and freshly ground black pepper
15 g butter medium onion finely chopped	4 tbsp double cream

Pre-heat the oven to 200 °C. Simmer the parsnips in salted water for 3 minutes. Drain well then add half the parmesan cheese. Pour olive oil into a roasting pan and heat in the oven for 3-4 minutes. Arrange the parsnips in the roasting pan, add the butter and bake for 45 minutes basting frequently. Drain any excess oil into a large saucepan and cook the onion gently without colouring until soft. Stir in the flour and cook for 1 minute. Add the stock, stirring constantly and bring to the boil. Add the parsnips and simmer covered for 10 minutes.

Liquidise the soup with the remaining parmesan cheese until smooth. Stir in the cream, season to taste then reheat.

Serves 6

Highlights

Art of a Garden

Monique's affinity with art is exhibited everywhere, not only in the design of the garden, the curves and the angles of the topiary and the metalwork, but in the sculptures that complement it. A real standout feature of the garden is the arbour on the terrace—its clever use of stained glass provides a colourful window between the gardens and the fields beyond.

Great Big Hairy Balls

The topiary is an obvious highlight—the spirals, the maze-like Knot Garden and, especially, the balls. Great big balls of...box. They look like giant green afros and give me an alarming desire to want to wobble them. And they do wobble beautifully, but please don't risk it; head gardener Paul will not be impressed.

Food, Glorious Food

All simply delicious and some great dishes for veggies. How could you resist anything with a name like Best Ever Fruit Cake? The recipes on this page are just a taster of the garden's culinary treats—see the Bourton House website for more, or better still, try something appetising whilst at the garden (no washing up involved!). Monique explains, 'I like to offer others what I personally like to enjoy when I go out, so that's been very much our criterion.' Perhaps Brewsters, Little Chef *et al.* should be taking notes...

Bourton House Garden, Bourton-on-the-Hill, Gloucestershire, GL56 9AE, 01386 700754
www.bourtonhouse.com

Picture Details

Most of the pictures featured in this book can be purchased as prints on photographic quality paper or in the framed Giclee format (canvas wrap). Enquiries can be made via our website www.theheartofagarden.com or by telephone 01326 3766064.

Key: The pictures are listed by page number and in order of appearance, top to bottom, left to right. The number in brackets after the picture/flower details identifies the postion on the page. See the image below as an example of how the pictures are numbered.

We've tried our best to make sure the information contained is correct; but if you're a bit of a smarty pants and have spotted errors, please kindly let us know so we can rectify them for the future.

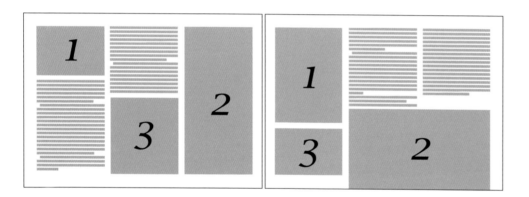

Stourton House Flower Garden

Abbey House Gardens

Selected Resources

Attenborough, David, *Life on Air,* BBC Books, 2002

Brickell, Christopher (Editor-in-chief), *The Royal Horticultural Society Encyclopedia of Plants and Flowers,* Dorling Kindersley, 2006

Drower, George, *Gardeners, Gurus & Grubs: The Stories of Garden Inventors & Innovations,* Sutton Publishing, 2001

Gibbons, Bob, *Field Guide to Insects of Britain and Northern Europe,* The Crowood Press, 1995

Hewitt, Terry, *The Complete Book of Cacti & Succulents,* Dorling Kindersley, 1993

Hitching, Judith, *A Guide to Garden Visits,* Michael Joseph Ltd, 1999

Memory Paterson, Jacqueline, *A Tree in Your Pocket,* Thorsons, 1998

Murphy, Graham, *Wildflowers,* National Trust Enterprises LTD, 2004

Reader's Digest, The, *Book of British Birds,* Drive Publications Limited, 1985

Rice, Graham, *The Gardener's Guide to Perennials,* Mitchell Beazeley, 1996

Sterry, Paul, *Complete British Wildflowers,* HarperCollins Publishers Ltd, 2006

Websites:

www.bbc.co.uk/gardening
www.wildaboutbritain.co.uk. Has a very useful forum.
www.helpfulgardener.com. Also an invaluable resource because of its forum.

A Special Thank You

Dick & Sue Bedrossian

Thank You

Glenn J. Boyle, Ph.D – proof reading and more.
John Gaunt – the IT Workshop
Pippa, Miranda, Kathy and all at Cornwall Film
Ben, Allyson, Dawn and all at Unlocking Cornish Potential
Russ Williams, Sam Coles and Tracey Stone at Oscha
Susan Pickett
Jim Craddock
Don and Doris Medlock
Chris and Pat Ovenden
Malcolm & Jacky Anker
Tom & Sue Gaunt
Dave & Sheila Brooks
Wayne and Denise Shaw
Martin's Mum and Dad aka Esther and Ron
Isaac, Sam and Josh
Molly – the Border Collie

The Film

This book is accompanied by two DVDs narrated by Richard Briers and featuring all sixteen gardens. You can buy a copy from the gardens themselves, or alternatively contact us for a list of retailers. A mail-order facility is also available.

If you enjoyed the book, the films will provide you with a great many more images across the seasons. Also, it provides an opportunity to meet some of the people behind the gardens. Should you then decide to visit these gardens, you will find enclosed with the film a booklet full of vouchers that will more than compensate the cost of purchase.

For sales or more details: www.theheartofagarden.com Telephone 01326 376064

Produced with the support of

CORNWALL FILM

This project is part-financed by the European Union

The Objective One Partnership for Cornwall & the Isles of Scilly

Working with Objective One